WHITENESS MADE SIMPLE

stepping into the GREY zone

William (Lez) Henry

Foreword by Colin King

LBC

Learning By Choice

WHITENESS MADE SIMPLE

ISBN 0955409417

First published 2007 by Nu-Beyond Ltd: Learning By Choice! PO Box 39266, Blackheath, London, SE3 8XQ, UK

A cataloguing in Publication Data record for this book is available from the British Library

www.nubeyond.com

Livications

To the Mother/Father/Male/Female Creation Principle that is responsible for all things in and at all times: Amen-Ra-Amen. One Blessed love to Miss Dotty (Earth Mother) who taught me to judge people by their actions and not their skin colour and to Sweet Sixteen (Earth Father) who taught me to stand up as a proud black man. To the Ancestors who saw fit to choose me as a vessel for Afrikan liberation in this dread time.

To my dearest little sister, Auntie June, who is the bravest and most loving human being I have met and if I was half as strong as you, I would have achieved twice as much. Love always, Bruv!

To my children, my family and my friends I give my thanks for your continued support for you make me whole.

To all who were kind enough to share their innermost thoughts on whiteness for inclusion in this piece and to the B.L.A.K. FRIDAY family; one perfect love!

To Dr. Marimba Ani, as from the moment I attended your London lecture in 1994, and purchased YURUGU, you opened my eyes to whiteness as an anti-human presence in the world and greatly assisted me on my 'academic' journey.

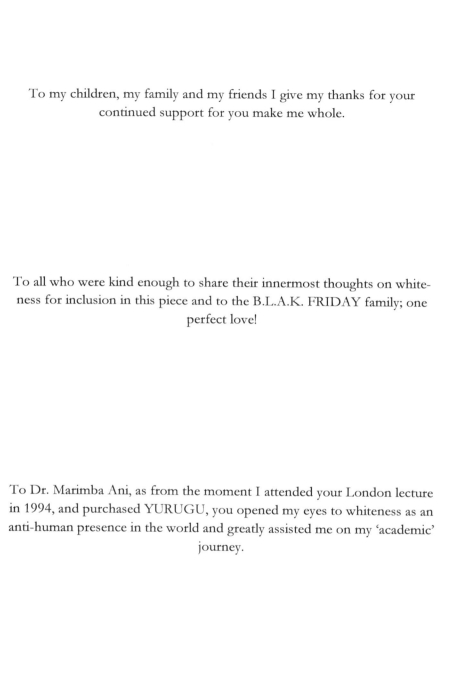

To Araya my blessed granddaughter in the hope that life is better for us all when you are grown.

To my wife Marlene; my debt to you cannot be described in words.

This book is not for you if you believe in ideas of natural superiority or inferiority based on:

The observable external (phenotypic) differences between the various members of the human family who are categorised as belonging to specific races.

Gendered differences in this sense being born male or female.

WHITENESS MADE SIMPLE

Class in the sense that the social position you are born into is a key determinant in your levels of intelligence

This book is for you if you:

Do not accept things just because someone in a position of 'authority' instructs you to do so.

Wish to consider the role that culture, in this sense patterns of behaviour created by humans, plays in the way we perceive self and other in a racist, white dominated, world.

Wish to understand the history and legacy of chattel enslavement and how it directly impacts on the present. For instance, a fact of this history is that the white-man name of the author of this book (see front cover) is a constant reminder (a memorial) that something was done to people who look like him (see back cover), that once understood will fully explain why you are reading his words in this place and at this time.

Appreciate the difference between the 'freedom to speak', and the 'freedom of speech' and Overstand that knowledge gives us the power to liberate or enslave!

WHITENESS MADE SIMPLE

Foreword

Dogmatic, rhetorical, seeking martyrdom and the corruption of the data to reinforce a racist masculine version of the truth. These are the words and accusations that Dr. Henry will inevitably face in his crusade to divert our attentions to an analysis of whiteness, from the inside out, from the emotional to the objective, from the black to white as we journey into the GREY zone. Henry considers how academics have been persuaded to believe that you lose your objective status if you reveal how your analysis has been affected by the evidence you see, feel and hear. Henry's challenge, in this new revolutionary book, is the methodological task of using his experiences as a mirror to reveal the pain of the past and current forms of racism exacted through whiteness.

To use a metaphor imagine whiteness lying inside its coffin, and the inhibitions that it enforces on those who attend its funeral but fail to speak honestly about the atrocities and the violations of its past. Henry conducts a ceremony to examine the invisibility of whiteness and what it constitutes on a number of highly insightful and powerful levels, from its birth in the demolition of African societies, its post-colonial life in places like the Caribbean, to its neo-colonial recreation in modern Britain. This notion is captured profoundly in the visual tensions witnessed in the moment where Henry is standing next to what has been historically constructed as the image of Jesus Christ.

Henry attempts in this book, or more pertinently what might be referred to as his attempt at 'academic' suicide because of the potential threat to his 'professional' credibility, to reveal what has been made invisible in the elevation of whiteness as a tool of oppression. His mission therefore, and he succeeds, is to present an intervention, based on a lived experience that has implications for our internal subliminal lives. He gives us comprehensive notes on the essence of whiteness, as an organic state, with functional parts, which camouflages its power to threaten those who make it visible; causing the emotional death of those who collude with its intrusion.

Henry represents the new cultural artist from the introduction to the last chapter, sculpturing whiteness, transforming it from fiction to fact through a graphic series of human interactions that are seldom revealed; simply because 'we don't want to go there'. His analysis prompts the move from cold scientific neutrality as he connects human tragedies and historical legacies, thus making whiteness not only simple, but conscious to those who have made it unconscious and un-connected. Moreover, as the racial therapist he deals with issues that affect all of us, stressing that we should all question the taken for granted nature of what whiteness is, and how it has impacted upon our lives. I know that as a black man, approaching middle age with a history of being misdiagnosed with schizophrenia, I recognise what has rescued me from suicide and given me the power to never give in and accept white pathology. I therefore welcome Henry's clarity and passion to make sense of whiteness and do something for the positive psychological health of black people.

The uniqueness of the book is that it elevates and celebrates our best and most profoundly powerful cultural therapists, Rodney, Welsing, hooks and Gilroy, who assist Henry in the task of enabling all of us, whether Africans or Europeans, to claim a refreshingly new, open, and liberating philosophical approach to the issue of white privilege. His hard hitting book has the potential to unify as opposed to continually polarise and divide. This unification is not based on the illusion of whiteness as the collective faith that embraces humanity under its assumed superiority. It is, as Henry describes, based on a new approach to our collective socialisation in racial differences, which challenges the way we interpret the past. Therefore, whilst the term 'white supremacy' is used, it is a narrative appraisal of how this concept can be used to detect arrest and investigate whiteness in zones of lived drama.

Henry's argument is a rare attempt in the history of social thought, by a black scholar, to analyse the supremacy of whiteness that has developed as a force, but remains hidden because of the reluctance of those who benefit from it to confess their sins. This is evidenced throughout this work, but is specifically dealt with in chapter 7, where he explains how himself, his family and generations of displaced Africans are still affected by whiteness and it's potential ability to kill, to destroy or lead us to deliberate self harm; culturally, politically and economically . What is then revealed and explained is his resilience and ability to resist his own cultural death, as he tells us exactly how he feels when confronted with black people who contribute to their own racial suicide. He also offers the idea of being 'too black for your own good'; detailing the stories of his teaching, the challenges of the words he uses in his lyrics, and the painful experiences of being a resident inside the insensitivity of British whiteness.

Henry's sophistication is to offer an argument that the idea of the 'GREY zone' is not about simply seeing race and whiteness as one dimensional, but as a uniquely challenging tool to analyse the complex unfolding post-modernist mask that enables us to really see the realities of our past and the future prospects of our cultural worlds. More critically the white imagination is encouraged to remove itself from being the prisoner of its methodological past, to liberate itself in the 'GREY zone' and so re-define and re-construct the other as the basis of making whiteness visible and transparent. This transparency is demonstrated when Henry makes sense of his life inside English whiteness through this process of deconstructing whiteness, of 're-writing reality', inside the black imagination. Consequently the special quality of the book is its attempt to demonstrate how white privilege, as a form of repression, has become a form of permanent cultural constipation which many whites suffer from because of their inability, or unwillingness to let it go. That is why the book's elevation of the black imagination is a really crucial attempt to enable groups of people, communities, and families of the Afrikan Diaspora to reclaim the power of self reliance and self definition inside the 'Grey Zone'.

Dr. Colin King. London, England, 2007

Table of Contents

Introduction: Simple things

> Throughout history, it has been the inaction of those who could have acted, the indifference of those who should have known better, the silence of the voice of justice when it mattered most, that has made it possible for evil to triumph. H.I.M. Haile Selassie I

It was my intention to write a book on whiteness that interrogated what white scholars had to say on the matter of white power/privilege from a black perspective. For this reason over the past few years I have read voraciously, researched doggedly and written copiously for the literature review, whilst bouncing my thoughts off various trustworthy people to ensure that my reasonings were intellectually rigorous. Then one day I remembered the above quote from His Imperial Majesty, and it dawned on me that if I pursued this matter in the tried and trusted 'academic' fashion my book would not be much different from what is already out there. It would have ended up being a generic dialogue with a bunch of white social commentators on what life is like for black people in their world. Similarly I would have no doubt found myself, due to my 'academic training', adhering to various Eurocentric conventions with regards to: What constitutes acceptable knowledge? How reliable are the sources of said knowledge? How said knowledge is ordered to substantiate my claims? What framework/methodology will be used to render my argument? In other words presenting what 'can' be objectively 'proven' and 'accepted', within the hallowed halls of academia, simply means presenting the opposite of how I really feel about being an Afrikan/black in a Eurocentric/white world; emotionally, racially, spiritually and psychologically.

The truth of the matter is that this is exactly how whiteness, as a way of bestowing kudos on white scholarship, works to the detriment of black scholars who are not afraid to be subjective and use their own cultural resources. Take a cursory glance at any text in a field, dominated by white scholars (anything familiar here), that seeks to define whiteness and see what sources they rely on to argue their main points. I guarantee that the works of any Afrikan who is regarded as 'threatening' is more often than not overlooked, or dealt with in a manner that perpetuates certain stereotypes about Black Nationalism from a Pan-Afrikan perspective. Consequently the former works of Marcus Mosiah Garvey or the present works of Minister Louis Farrakhan epitomise this form of strategic avoidance, as they are seldom considered as 'valid' sources of knowledge. That is why their 'inclusion' is usually accompanied by disparaging remarks by those who wish to keep all of us confused. This happens for no other reason than they uncompromisingly speak of the need for a black revolutionary consciousness; suggesting blacks should put 'Race First', which is what most white people do anyway, for that is the ultimate gift of whiteness as it makes such behaviour appear normal and natural.

I think it is inhumanly arrogant and insulting when Europeans, who have primarily 'taught' non-Europeans what it means to be non-European, think they can still tell 'us' who can present an argument on 'our' behalf. More so when so many fail to appreciate what is truly at stake in discussions about racism or white privilege? For instance, if I had a pound for every conversation I have had with white people who freely use the word 'denigrate', I would be a very rich man. That is why I point out to them that the word can literally mean to turn into a nigger; it is more than a mere disparaging remark, it represents a dehumanising historical process. Look up the definitions of the word and amongst them you will find the traits and characteristics associated with the Negro; who was without doubt the product of a historical process. Likewise I was told that slave masters often used the term as a sign of total disrespect when quarrelling with each other. I wonder how many white people are aware of this mundane fact which explains why racism permeates all aspects of their supremacist cultures.

Similarly how many whites feel sad or depressed when exposed to advertising campaigns that readily encourage 'us' to trace 'our' family tree? Do they reach for their cheque books to take up a great offer to access their lineage, or do they reach for the tissues knowing that for many Afrikans our 'family tree' too often had 'Strange Fruit' suspended from the branches? That is why the case of the Jena 6 in the USA is so damned depressing where it is reported that:

> Last fall, when two Black high school students sat under the "white" tree on their campus, white students responded by hanging nooses from the tree. When Black students protested the light punishment for the students who hung the nooses, District Attorney Reed Walters came to the school and told the students he could "take [their] lives away with a stroke of [his] pen." (http://jena6.vesana.com/thecase)

Consider being faced with these terror tactics in this day and age and then if ever asked 'what role is there for whites' or 'what can a white person do, if anything?' (Back & Ware 2002:148/151), tell them this. Our racialised reality is not a joke, nor is our barbaric treatment by whites an accident of fate, it is ongoing, deliberate and will not be addressed by relying on the views of 'safe' blacks and unrealistic whites. Take heed of what black people who are not afraid to speak are telling you about yourselves and your role in our ongoing struggles against white supremacy. Learn to scrape off the veneer of 'whiteness as rightness', that which has blinded and bedevilled the majority of the human family for far too long now. In other words the 'invisible hand' of destiny, that intangible 'god-like' presence that has privileged whites and made their assumed superiority the norm, needs to be made visible.

The way I intend to do so in this book will probably offend/upset many people of all so-called races especially, I hope, many white people who need to accept that the 'white way' is seldom the 'right way', to do things. I believe they need to wake up to the reality of their power position which will, if it remains unchecked, ultimately destroy this planet and all life on it. For this reason I present here a series of reasonings that can be read in any order as they are not based on the tried and trusted linear, orthodox, approach to a 'rational' argument. They are based on my thoughts and reflections on various aspects of racial inequality, that whilst often tackling many issues that affect other non-Europeans—we do indeed often share the experience of European aggression via imperialism and colonialism—is written from the perspective of an Afrikan who is not afraid to be black in a whitened world. This is because whilst there are similarities with oppressed others, there are distinct differences in the experiences of Afrikans, which will become apparent throughout this journey into my quest for social justice.

The book features an introduction, which you are presently engaged with, four essays and four collections that I entitle 'Witnesses to whiteness: making the invisible, visible'. These collections feature pieces I have written for various outlets, as well as the thoughts of a few people I asked one basic question: what does whiteness mean to you? Herein you will find their answers to this pressing concern, all of which show the breadth of opinion that generally occurs when the concept of whiteness is discussed in an open and honest way. The essays on the other hand deal with four specific areas of concern that I believe need to be considered in any argument on racial inequality as it impacts on black life. In chapter 3, 'Sociology in the GREY zone', I consider the role white social theorists have played in undermining a pro-black perspective, by using their conventional racialised yardstick to measure the worth of black scholarship. That is why the GREY zone is a space that many white commentators know exists, but fail to acknowledge its existence, because it would mean taking a long hard look in the mirror and recognising how complicit they are in the systematic racial, spiritual, cultural, political and social destruction of people who do not look like them.

In chapter 5, 'Too black for your own good: Head-Decay-Shun', I explain why you cannot expect your enemy to 'educate' you when their system was not designed for your upward social mobility. For instance, once coincidence is placed to one side, how can we explain the fact that black boys are up to six times more likely to be excluded from school than their white peers for exactly the same offence? Or how could one of my daughters finish top of her primary school—and it turns out she had the best marks out of all the new entrants to her secondary school—and yet mysteriously end up in the third highest class at secondary school? I seek answers to these questions and drawing on black cultural resources offer a template for overcoming this aspect of living in Babylon.

In chapter 7, 'Ah-Free-Ka: combating whiteness in the black imagination', I consider the process of the white-washing of the black mind that is one of the constants in European aggression against Afrikan people. I argue that the ancient Afrikans under-stood that for the human being to be healthily balanced, the mind and the body had to be fed accordingly. The Ka is the 'life force' that distinguishes the 'dead' from the 'living' person and my argument is that many Afrikans are psychologically 'dead' and in desperate need of an antidote to the poisonous Eurocentric diet our minds consume on a daily basis.

Chapter 9, 'Crouching niggers, hidden crackers: we're in a 'white' mess-iah' (Iah means Rasta) is based on a series of talks I have been delivering for a few years now entitled 'Ah weh dem ah gwaan wid? Challenging blackassassination in the media and on tell-lie-vision'. In the talks I expose the history behind some of the tactics that are used to brainwash Afrikans into worshiping Europeans, and draw on an array of 'popular' and 'unpopular' sources to make my argument. I always explain that if you use the term 'nigger' to describe Afrikans then you should use the word 'cracker' to describe Europe-ans, because these terms are the opposite sides of the same historical coin. The 'niggers' were the dehumanised, chattel enslaved Africans who were often crouching under the yoke of the brutal masters who generally administered the lash. Consequently the onomatopoeic crack of the whip became synonymous with them in the minds of enslaved Africans, hence the perfect name for them; 'crackers'. But sometimes the person who whipped you looked like you, merely doing their 'job', whilst the 'cracker' who controlled them remained behind the scenes safely 'hidden' from public view.

This is still the case as evidenced in a damning indictment from Robert Beckford, taken from a documentary about the continued exploitation of Afrikans in Ghana by European multinational companies, which we know affects all of the continent.

> When I heard the stories being told this morning I thought to myself. This is; they are treated like niggers. That's the only way you can describe how these Afrikan people are being treated. You cannot say to me that these people are considered to be human beings, with feelings, with emotions, with values, with something worth living for. Because the way they are being treated here; I haven't got words for it. The only word that you can use is that they have been made to be and live like niggers. People who are less than human beings. (Beckford, 2007)

When daring to openly discuss the prickly subject of how black people ended up in this predicament, we cannot separate ourselves from the terror tactics that were used to break our will. One such tactic manifests in the reality that no matter how badly white people treat some Africans, they still look to them for salvation. I will therefore wade through the rhetoric and explain why the brothers and sisters Beckford spoke of are me; if I ended up where they are I would be treated the same and for this reason we have to look at what global forces are marshalled against Afrikan people to keep us mentally and physically enslaved. I will therefore question the notion of worshipping a white Jesus by revealing how such imagery is used to colonise the consciousness of Afrikan people. On many occasions when I have done so I have had black Christians of all denominations condemn me, verbally abuse me, and even pray for my salvation because 'satan mussi ah ride mi'.

That is why in this chapter I contemplate how something that is so central to Afrikan people/black people, which is our belief in the divine, is used by the 'hidden crackers' as the greatest weapon against us. Thus be warned that for me there are no 'sacred cows', because my thoughts on whiteness can be summed up in the few words a youth once said to me whilst reasoning in Jamaica: "if man an woman mek it? Man an woman can defeat it."

Witnesses to whiteness: making the invisible, visible

> Whiteness is Worldness. **Anon**

> **The Plastic Smile**
> The plastic smile is used to beguile the purity of mind.
> The plastic smile is used to confuse
> people who have been subjected to racial abuse.
> The plastic smile conceals callous thoughts,
> the projector of which disacknowledges prejudice...
> but that plastic smile is here to stay,
> because it has been ingrained that way.
> **Myrna Loy**

London, United Kingdom, 1988

As the result of a telephone conversation, during which I convinced the other person that my credentials, experience, and the reputable firms I had worked for as a self employed central heating engineer, were more than adequate to be employed by his company, I was offered a job. I left Southeast London and drove to Tonbridge in Kent (approximately a one and a half hour journey) to begin my contract and arrived at a housing estate at 7.45am for an 8am start as agreed. Many who are reading this will probably, and quite rightly, be thinking I know what's coming next as once my prospective white employer saw my black face he couldn't hide his shock, horror and obvious disappointment. He then, once he evolved beyond making guttural sounds and had fully recovered the power of speech, beckoned for me to follow him around the building site. He then explained that he did not mean for me to start work immediately as he was not sure what work he had and that the jobs were for a two man team. Now me being the reasoned and rational person that I am, I stopped him outside one of the flats and asked him to explain, quite simply, why he did not tell me this when we spoke at length on the phone. I further explained that I had neither time nor petrol to waste and suggested that maybe he did not wish to employ me because I am black. Those who know me are aware that I have a voice that carries, even when I am not shouting, and for this reason a white guy I had worked with on a previous site named Pete came out and greeted me. He then suggested that I could 'two's up' (pair up) with him to do the installations as he was working on his own.

What happens next? Did I ask the white man who had been lying to me for however long to explain why Pete could be employed in this way but I obviously couldn't? The answer is I never had another conversation with him but worked with Pete on various sites for that company. I remember trying to explain to Pete that the guy was racist and I am familiar with this type of behaviour, having experienced it throughout my life. Pete, being immersed in whiteness thought I was overreacting or just plain paranoid until he witnessed something for himself a few months later. We were central heating bungalows in a place called Deal in Kent and decided to stay in 'digs' (bed and breakfast accommodation) as it was more cost effective than commuting every day. We had been working there for a few weeks when one evening we were driving around and saw a snooker hall and decided to go inside and play a few games. I was driving and dropped Pete outside the entrance and proceeded to find a space to park the car. By the time I had done so and went into the snooker hall Pete had set up the balls on the table and was ready to play. However, before I even got to him the white guy behind the counter shouted "excuse me, are you a member? You need to be a member to play in here." I looked at him and pointed to Pete and said "is he a member?" The guy behind the counter told Pete that he "mistook him for one of their regulars and he is sorry but we will both have to leave." Pete was visibly shocked and began to argue with the guy, but I told him it was cool and let's just leave as I don't have time for this foolishness.

Similarly in 2002 when I was tutor at Goldsmiths College, I and a fellow white male colleague were teaching as part of a summer school project, when a student needed the bathroom as we walked through the student's union building. Whilst we waited my colleague began to play a piano that was in the lobby and within seconds a white woman came out of her office, totally ignored my colleague, and asked me "what do you think you're doing?" I gave no reply but my colleague said to her "why are you talking to Lez when I am the one playing the piano?" She did not answer but simply turned and left and my colleague could not believe what he had witnessed.

There are two main reasons why I did not actively pursue these occurrences; the first, in a word, is temper. I know what mine is like and I had to weigh up whether these bigoted by-products of a racist society and imagination were worth the aggravation, had I really got into it with them. They were not. The second is because I am fully aware that their behaviour is a necessary consequence of our collective socialisation. For these types it is natural to be white; it is natural for them to be white and oppress blacks; and it will remain so until the day they are slapped with the black truth of their condition. This is why black folk are the best witnesses to whiteness, because white folk don't seem to get what is at stake when merely trying to 'live', whilst being black, in their world. **W. Henry**

Whiteness = A perceived notion of a "universal standard" for which all good things are judged, is based on a lie supported by ideological propaganda/warfare, for which there appears to be no escape!!!! Power to the Conscious...**Sister Panyin**

Whiteness and its notions of superiority if it is anything is the ideological refuge of the scared and insecure…attempting to convince but alas condemned to fail and be forever fragile. **Dr. Perry Stanislas**

Introduction

> A "Black Social Theory" will lead us out of the Whiteness of Eurocentric madness and into the Blackness of African salvation. Bobby E. Wright

> I sing sociology. So right here you will find your identity! Hollis "Chalkdust" Liverpool

> To transcend the downpression the black race ah face, haffi recognise our Afrikan base, that ah Afrikan roots from an Afrikan race, who were spread like butter all over the place, treatment we get it was a big disgrace, treated like pieces of human waste, speak yuh own language kick innah yuh face, rebel gainst the master you gone without trace, even nowadays nuff of the white race, we roots an we culture nuh want we fi trace, cau armed with the truth you are a big threat, that's why them talk bout forgive an forget, them can tell that foolishness to I and you, but them wouldn't dare try tell that to a Jew, cau Jews tell the world everyday weh God send, remember the past "NEVER AGAIN." (Lezlee Lyrix, Afrikan Body, White Man Mind, 1994)

I suggest in the lyrical extract above that if you arm yourself with 'truth' you represent a 'big 'threat' to those who wish to deny you a counteractive voice. For once you have an alternative idea of 'truth' you are in a position to challenge what constitutes 'acceptable knowledge' and take people into the GREY zone. That space where lived experience outweighs 'scientific objectivity' in the quest for answers to vexed questions. On occasions when I have done so, I have been informed by fellow sociologists that I am 'too emotional' or 'too close to the subject to be objective'. I actually take such comments as compliments because firstly, 'I use this thing called "strategic bias"…Everyone is biased against us, so why can't we do it? I don't go for spurious claims of objectivity. I just say "this is it – this is my version of it" (Henry/Eden, 'Woofah Magazine', 2007:2). Secondly, it shows that I have not compromised my humanness: that which drives me to solve problems in the real world as a member of the human family.

Every day in some way human beings experience and contemplate our social predicament and whether the end result is ecstasy or depression, we regularly draw on an array of sources in our endeavours to make life make sense. We thus have here a great example of applied sociological thinking, which means in our efforts to understand the social we 'live' and breathe 'sociology'. Or as Chalkdust reminds us, when we utilise counter-cultural spaces to express our heartfelt concerns in our quests to unpack racialised identities, we 'sing sociology'. What then needs to be explained is how this type of thinking differs from sociology as a discipline which has been used as a weapon against black communities who are measured by the gaze of white sociologists. What generally happens is 'we' (black folk) become the next project to various funded social researchers, who quite often do not have a visceral investment in the futures of the communities in question. Thus in line with Ani (1994) I believe:

> ...the most important source is my own experiences of the culture. Experiencing the intellectual core through its academies, feeling the weight of its oppression through my Africanness, I have been both semiparticipant and "observer," amassing evidence of the nature of European reality through direct confrontation. The advantage of being African is that it has allowed me to penetrate European culture form a "non-European" frame of reference. (Ani 1994:10)

I will therefore consider how the black presence in the UK became the object of scrutiny under the academic gaze, during a time when many theorists tried to analyse this 'alien' presence through the lens of the sociology of race. Without perhaps considering that the tools of analysis they were using were fatally flawed, the by-products of a white racist imagination that sought to rationalise, record, and re-present the social world in their own Eurocentric image. I will also make known the shaping effects of science and colonialism that are central to understanding our contemporary situation, because both have played a critical role in how the black 'other' becomes known to the white 'self'. As will become evident the only way to truly over-stand why Afrikan/black people are deliberately misrepresented in contemporary British society, is to understand the history of ideas that fuels such gross misrepresentations and equally how they can be resisted and transcended.

On sociological misunderstandings

Much has been written on the impact the arrival of the 'Windrush generation' had on the indigenous white communities in the UK from the late 1940s. Particularly in the context of the overt racism these Caribbean migrants faced and the cultural misunderstandings that took place on both sides. Indeed there was an assumption that both parties had an idea of what to expect from the other, after all they were British subjects. However, the truth is that the Caribbean migrants were really an unknown quantity in the UK and the majority of the white population had very little contact with black people (and many still don't to this very day). That is why the particularities of the lifestyles they knew and obviously transported with them when they came to the 'mother country', for a short term 'visit', became highly problematic. This meant that the cultural, religious, political and social sensibilities that they took for granted—that which all members of the human family use as a template for existence in a rudimentary sense—were deemed to be at best bizarre, more so when we consider the migrants inter-island variations in customs and speech. More importantly, it was simply the colour of their skin that was most threatening to many of the ordinary white citizens they came in contact with on a daily basis.

A possible way to understand this occurrence was that the white working class people, who blacks invariably ended up living tooth to jowl with, had little if any practical knowledge of the lifestyles of these 'dark strangers' (Patterson, 1964). Having little meaningful contact with blacks meant that their ideas of black life were based on a commonsense, racialised, understanding of what they 'knew' about these 'others'. Similarly, more often than not, this was the same for the blacks who came to Britain, so a really important point for us to consider here is where did their knowledge of each other come from? One way I will suggest is through popular cultural forms such as films that glorified the British Empire and the correctness of 'civilised' white domination of 'uncivilised' non white others. A factor that Young suggests occurred when:

> During the 1920s, Britain's Colonial Office decided to exploit the propaganda qualities of film as it set out to explore how best to capitalize on cinema's potential for disseminating imperial ideology. There was a concern that some of the images of white people could be interpreted as deriding European or British culture…and eventually such texts were censored for screenings in the colonies. (Young, 1996:66)

Sociology in the GREY zone

Young's observation allows us to think about how this form of colonial propaganda impacted on the black and white communities who would be exposed to these forms of racist propaganda. Firstly it provided a template for many white people to 'know' these colonised others and firmly appreciate where their placement in the world should be which is 'out there', somewhere in the colonies as the subjects of 'our' rule. Secondly it deluded many white people into believing they knew what to expect when those who were ruled 'out there' were 'invited' to come over here to assist in the rebuilding of the mother country after the Second World War. What then became problematic for the white majority was when these blacks, more often than not, failed to act out the stereotypical roles that myriad forms of media propaganda had readied them to expect. In fact members of the black communities often found themselves faced with difficult situations that were the result of cultural misunderstandings with the dominant white community, where their ordinary behaviour was often interpreted as bizarre and unwelcome. For instance:

> Patterson identified a cultural gap between the newcomers and hosts, in spite of superficial similarities of language and religion. In Brixton, the white population largely upheld 're-spectable' norms which stress, privacy, 'keeping themselves to themselves', cleanliness and tidiness, quietness and family propriety. But, she pointed out, 'No immigrant group has in the mass so signally failed to conform to these expectations

> and patterns as have the West Indians. The newcomers tend to be noisy and gregarious, less fastidious about housekeeping standards, and they had a higher proportion of common-law marriages. These departures from 'normal' expectations inevitably caused tensions between the two communities. (Richardson and Lambert 1985:33)

This is not the place for me to discuss the obvious cultural distortions and myopia that underpins Patterson's account of black family life, where 'the onus is upon black 'immigrants' to assimilate' (Graham 2002:38). Rather I will argue that her 'observations' about the 'West Indians' obvious 'failure to conform to these expectations' reflect the way that black communities are still regarded in contemporary British society. Far more importantly, her observations were underpinned by a racist assumption that the cultures of those from the colonies were inferior when compared to those of the 'white population'. What this means is the specificity of the cultural tools and frameworks that people use to make sense out of their environment are regarded as superficial aberrations that can only be understood through the lens of the dominant culture. Equally this is what has happened to discussions about racism which specifically affects non-white people in general, and Afrikan/black people in particular. Racism has now become confused with discriminatory practices and we therefore need to consider what racism is and also what, in my opinion, racism is most definitely not.

Sociology in the GREY zone

Overstanding racism

For quite a while now I have been delivering staff training sessions to both private and public organisations on what I call 'Diversity Management'. One aspect of the training deals with the notion of racism and I begin by asking all in attendance if they understand what racism is. Invariably they will suggest that racism is a system of oppression based on the classification of the members of the human family into distinct races based on phenotypic (external) appearance. However, once we start to interrogate their assumptions, it is amazing how many times we have ended up with a 'race' of 'Gypsies, Italians, Jews, gays and lesbians'. This type of 'racial' confusion I think is deliberate and necessary to a society that refuses to have a mature discussion about its racist foundation. That is why we are constantly fed one type of distraction after another in the mainstream where all of the above can be white and in conflict with one another, yet claim to be racially abused by members of their own race.

I mention this because it is the only way to make sense of the imminent death of the Commission for Racial Equality (CRE) and its replacement with the Commission for Equality and Human Rights (CEHR). What will inevitably happen is that the historical reasons that peoples of Afrikan ancestry are in the global position they are in now will be obscured by a one size fits all solution to social inequalities.

WHITENESS MADE SIMPLE

Have you ever noticed that on the few occasions when issues are raised that specifically deal with the MAAFA, in the mainstream, they invariably get reduced to human rights issues? More so this year, 2007, when the Government and their lackeys have been ramming the 'Wilberfest' down our throats and collapsing chattel enslavement, human trafficking and other forms of un-freedom into a campaign for 'social justice'. I have since January 2007 delivered a series of talks entitled 'Fighting The Wilberfarce' on behalf of various organisations, a few secondary schools and, thanks to the conscious Batwa Seaton brothers and sisters, I delivered one such talk in Bermuda. I have done so for one main reason which is to counter the 'intellectual' status of the 'official' representatives of the sanitised version of the 'Abolition of the "slave-trade" Act of 1807'. Fortunately, this has provided me with the opportunity to get into some public debates with some of these 'expert' historians, sociologists and anthropologists, which I invariably win because truth is they know almost nothing about the Afrikan presence before 'chattel enslavement'. More importantly, they don't have to know anything because the dominant view is that Afrikans made no contribution to anything of note.

Simply put that is how whiteness works in the favour of these 'experts' as it qualifies an idea of the oppressor as reasonable, without them ever addressing the specificities of how Afrikans came to be the dispossessed and disenfranchised 'white man's burden'. That is why I want to point out that I believe that much of what is done, and continues to be done, to peoples of Afrikan ancestry is racist, deliberate and necessary to a system that was founded on white supremacist thought and action. As such, there must be a healthy appreciation of the historical forces and circumstances that are largely responsible for us inheriting the racialised world that we now inhabit. In line with this perspective, Welsing offers what she terms a 'functional definition' of racism, which is:

> …the local and global power system structured and maintained by persons who classify themselves as white, whether consciously or subconsciously determined; this system consists of patterns of perception, logic, symbol formation, thought, speech, action and emotional response. (Welsing, 1991:ii)

Welsing makes known how problematic it is to analyse 'racism' and its impact on the lives of black people, without considering how those who 'classify' themselves as white control these 'local and global power systems'. Moreover to overlook the centrality of their role in normalising their privileged position, in this 'global power system', is to deny the reality of their dominant worldview. Of equal importance black communities should be mindful when white scholars whose 'race' is used as a measurement of what it means to be normal, valued and human, fail to consider that they, or their racial group, never have to measure up to such ideal types in the way that black people do. Although they may classify themselves as 'white', when they are commenting on racism as an aspect of domination, their own whiteness is seldom questioned or pathologised in the way blackness is, which means:

> We have been looking at the trees and ignoring the essential nature of the forest. The fact is that black people have been oppressed by a system unified on the basis of white racism. Racism is a concept that speaks to the total system, the essential nature of the social order as perceived by black people. (Alkalimat, 1998:176)

Alkalimat's observation is telling as he suggests that the best-qualified people to speak about the real effects of 'racism' are those on the receiving end. Hence if we are to think about what sociological analysis entails we have to question its 'values' in our endeavours to check out the 'nature of the forest'. The point is any attempt to determine how the notion of racism has become an integral part of our contemporary social reality, must consider the theoretical underpinnings of the sociology of race. This is necessary because such theorisations were, and still are, the templates for how the lives of black people are measured and then presented as 'truth'. What often happens is that the social relations of white society, class based or

otherwise, are used as the chief determinants in analysing the behavioural patterns of black families and individuals. Black people become the focus of 'problem oriented analysis' and that is why we can have ex Prime Minister Blair, in 2007, blaming us for every social ill that affects our children. Thus unsurprisingly with his myopic, whitened, version of this great country's historical past he suggests:

> We need to stop thinking of this as a society that has gone wrong - it has not - but of specific groups that for specific reasons have gone outside of the proper lines of respect and good conduct towards others and need by specific measures to be brought back into the fold. (Blair, 2007, http://news.bbc.co.uk frontpage/story)

Isn't it telling that Blair's comments have the same chilling undertones as those of our 'former masters', where 'proper lines of respect and good conduct' were whatever white supremacists deemed them to be? In fact for those of us who may mistakenly believe that things have changed, Blair's comments give us a timely reminder that:

> To the colonialist mind it was always of the utmost importance to be able to say: 'I know my natives', a claim which implied two things at once: (a) that the native was really quite simple and (b) that understanding him and controlling him went hand in hand – understanding being a pre-condition for control and control being adequate proof of understanding. (Achebe, 1988:48)

That is why Blair and his ilk's idea of the manner in which 'specific groups' need 'to be brought back into the fold', will not consider how said groups arrived in 'the fold', and have been deliberately 'folded' and structurally placed in positions of disadvantage. The historical legacies of chattel enslavement, imperialism, colonialism, that which Leary suggests has impacted us with 'Post traumatic Slave Syndrome' (2005), will be overlooked in a society that hasn't 'gone wrong'. Rather the 'specific groups' will be judged by a yardstick that is the measure of the 'others' (white people), who are, I suppose, the paragons of virtuous 'good conduct', because their methods of 'control' are based on the power to enforce their will.

Blair's perspective is not new and that is why the history behind this type of 'thinking' needs to be made clear to those who seek solutions to real problems, as the impact of racism on black lifestyles is seldom considered. In fact it has been documented that 'many behavioural scientists argue that Black families were no more than simply "sick" white families' (Nobles & Goddard 1984:3). This means that then, and now, in such instances any sense of cultural autonomy is denied to black families, because the 'traditional' ways of being that are used to resist and transcend white racism are regarded as "sick", thereby omitted or generally glossed over.

This perspective had and still has serious ramifications for the black communities who came to the UK during the period after the

Second World War, for in many ways it relegates their immediate concerns to 'the unreal or insubstantial, secondary or peripheral' (Gilroy 2000:98). Therefore whilst it is accepted 'that people do conceive of themselves and others as belonging to 'races' and do describe certain sorts of situation and relations as being 'race relations" (Miles 1982:42), these are in essence 'false constructions'. An idea that was challenged by Gilroy (1987) who argued:

> Miles therefore attacks black writers who have initiated a dialogue with Marxism over racism in Britain because they use 'race' in spite of its illusory status, to 'encourage' the formation of a particular political force…Miles describes racism and racialization as having 'autonomous but limited effects' but does not specify how much autonomy his own political strategy will cede to blacks in Britain. (Gilroy 1987:22)

Gilroy's comments, made nearly two decades apart, question the 'authority' of a form of scholarship that fails to recognise the worth of a 'politics of black autonomy', which would no doubt bestow a form of 'insider' ownership to black writers. I believe this is discouraged because with the collective support of a highly visible alternative, a cadre of black scholars in the UK, 'outsider' perspectives of a lived black reality would face a serious intellectual challenge. For if 'you' (white scholars) have the analytical tools to present 'our' story from the outside, then why shouldn't 'we' (black scholars) use the same tools to present 'our' story from the inside?

When this is not the case black scholars are subject to a 'political strategy' that manifests as racial, cultural and intellectual segregation, which blocks off avenues of meaningful dialogue with the dominant white society. Hence comments like Blair's shed light on why non-white groups in Britain are continually subjected to the negative labelling, stereotyping, and demeaning social positioning that constitute the everyday exercising of white superiority. Therefore a theory of race formation or 'race relations' must enable the interrogation of how 'unwitting' actions reproduce white privilege, thereby making institutionalised racism seem 'normal'. In fact according to Back 'I am not suggesting that institutional racism is monolithic or all pervasive. Rather I am concerned to identify the social locations where black people encounter racist ideologies and discourses' (Back 1996:162).

Back deals with one of the major concerns of the scholars who argue that not all white people are in powerful positions, therefore their influence upon 'racist ideologies and discourses' will be minimal. Back also explains that there are 'social locations where black people encounter', on a daily basis, the barriers that whiteness constructs for them that do not necessarily impact on normal class relations in the same way. This is because whiteness is said to 'be everything and nothing' as white people 'colonise the definition of the normal' (Dyer 1997:45/46). Moreover an analysis of the experiences of being disadvantaged for being born black produces knowledge of white dominance and privilege. But experiences of racialised privilege that seek to interrogate what it means to be white, discourages knowledge of collective privilege as white people can choose whether or not to acknowledge racism. Often times when they do acknowledge their complicity in perpetuating racism they will draw for the get out clause, I am an 'unwitting' participant, using Macintosh's 'invisible knapsack' (1989) as an excuse for an ongoing experience. Indeed they can step in or out of the GREY zone, wilfully or otherwise, safe in the knowledge that their whiteness protects them.

The suggestion is there is a qualitative difference between having an experience and not having it, and more so between having an experience repeatedly, based on the colour of your skin, and never having it at all. For instance, 'ethnic minorities' are seen as different and inferior due to ascribed racial differences, which are almost always reduced to phenotypic difference. Shared experiences of racialised inclusion or exclusion come from being treated as subordinated or privileged in a systemic sense. Thus it is the relationship between knowledge and power that needs to be considered because the effects of 'race' as 'truth' are produced within discourses, which are neither 'true' nor 'false'. We therefore need to mindful that all systems of knowledge, including sociological knowledge, are implicated in relations of power.

Seeking 'enlightenment': Unshackling the mind

The issues surrounding 'race' with regards to power and social divisions, represent a unique set of sociological problems, thereby opposing the suggestion that racism only arises out of present social conditions. The argument is that the social and historical factors that shape such beliefs should be investigated in their own right and proper context. So for instance if you are black, highly qualified with an impressive track record in your given field, and still find that in this day and age you are being discriminated against with regards to promotion or such like, it is pointless looking solely inward to find answers. Ignoring the manner in which the society you live in is structured along a racial hierarchy, where whiteness is valued and blackness is not, is tantamount to committing social suicide. In this type of analysis where understanding the effects of 'systemic' or 'institutionalised racism' is crucial to the outcome, there must be a focus on the historical particularities of the communities in question; for there is nothing simple about being black in British society' (John 2006:279).

John's suggestion is that we need an explanatory frame-work, from which we can dismiss matters of coincidence or the 'unwitting' actions of individual racists, and ascertain how certain beliefs have so much currency in contemporary British society. Otherwise we run the risk of reproducing the same line of argument that ignores the voices of those who are the main recipients of discriminatory practices, because 'people are trapped in history and history is trapped in people' (Baldwin, 1985:81). Consequently we must recognise that our ideas of history are what inform the present reality and as such we must be mindful that 'what people make of physical differences, the everyday or commonsense notions which influence them, constitutes the social meaning of race' (Richardson & Lambert 1985:16).

Utilising this aspect of 'social meaning', a serious challenge can be made as there is no 'scientific' evidence to support any notion of an inherent superiority or inferiority, premised on phenotypic difference, between the 'races'. Nevertheless, it is precisely because the concept of 'race' has no biological foundation and is therefore a constructed generalised ideal, that it can influence and often determine a group's 'social meaning' at any given moment. Furthermore, if we are honest, most of the recognised 'experts' on black cultures are non-black, which is a direct legacy of the manner in which black people have been studied, objectified, pathologised and then presented as the universal 'other', by anthropologists, sociologists and psychologists. As the late Garnett Silk, stated in his song 'Zion in a Vision' (1996):

> You regard us as animal our predecessors as cannibal, you say we came from the Ape but we know the truth so you are late, we know where we are going, and we know where we are from, so to hell with you, and your brainwash education'.

When you penetrate Silk's wise words on the historical and generational links between forms of 'social meaning' ascribed to the 'other', they beg the question: why should 'we' (blacks) have to enhance 'their' (whites) privileged position, when 'we' should in fact be fighting for 'our' 'own' recognition in 'our' struggles against white supremacy? Crucially then, the specificity of the historical experiences of the Afrikan/black communities, whose forefathers and foremothers were 'regarded as animals', needs to be considered. For it is suggested that 'colonialism took over where slavery left off, ensuring that our labour would continue to bolster and maintain the British economy for years to come' (Bryan, Dadzie & Scafe1985:10). Making these palpable historical links known enables us to appreciate why the Caribbean migrants who sought gainful employment upon their arrival in Britain, during the 1950s and 1960s, found that the kinds of work they were offered soon became known as 'black jobs'. The types of employment that would stymie their social mobility and stifle their aspirations:

> ...due to racism 'you couldn't get a civil servants job, or any job, in fact, that's commensurate with your education'. Dish-washing, assembly line work, streetsweeping, and other man-

> ual labouring jobs were taken by individuals trained to be teachers, accountants and administrators. Nursing was the main occupation into which women went; although this provided housing (in largely West Indian-occupied nurses' homes), training and a skilled profession, wages were poor, chances for promotion were minimal, and the duties given to the immigrants were the most undesirable. (Vertovec 1993:172)

Vertovec makes known how the system of oppression that ensured that black people inhabited the spaces that were assigned to them in the employment market in Britain, guaranteed that their structural placement was consistent with how the colonies were organised around the exploitation of black labour. A factor that makes even more sense when we realise that many of these West Indians ended up in the Britain due 'to the pressures placed on people to sell their land' (Campbell, 1986:86). Hence, whilst it is clear to appreciate that 'race' may not be 'real' with regards to marking biological differences, its consequences certainly are for the black communities who are left to combat its historical legacy.

We must therefore be prudent when evaluating the ramifications of a historical legacy that impacts on the manner in which we explain black life in the contemporary, because without taking these aspects into consideration the picture will remain biased and incomplete. More importantly, as previously stated, many of the 'experts' on black life are white researchers who analyse the black subject/object at a distance and once the interview is completed, the project is written up, or the computer is shut down for the day, they can safely retreat into their private comfort zone. This means that the cloak of whiteness that insulates many of them from the reality of the condition of the descendants of African chattel slaves is seldom questioned, except during those moments when they specifically challenge it under the guise of 'black or white studies'. Therefore, social scientists and other commentators should consider and acknowledge, especially if they are white, how much authority is placed on their accounts of the black experience in Britain. This is why 'race' poses so many epistemological problems for disciplines that claim to be 'scientific', because science cannot deal with a variable that promotes an acceptance of an 'imagined' natural 'difference'.

Consequently, in their endeavours to address these concerns, many sociologists and other social commentators have sought to 'provide' marginalized groups with a platform for debating alternative models of social, economic and political discourse. By recognising plurality they argue that 'the politics of difference, diversity and identity have given a new edge to demands for equality and social justice' (Meekosha 1993:172). In anthropology it is known as the 'reflexive turn', a way to reverse the ethnographic 'gaze', which supposedly creates a more balanced relationship between observer and participant as the narrative is produced by the former object of scrutiny. So you give the 'native' a video camera or tape recorder and say 'gwaan'! Go and capture your folk in their natural habitat and then we can 'write up' the findings 'together' to present a more 'authentic' account. Question is who controls the finished product and what political purposes will it be used for?

I would argue that this notion of capturing/celebrating difference in 'fragmented' Western societies 'has normalised a form of ghoulish separateness - a form of segregation which exists simultaneously with cosmopolitanism' (Harris, 1993:38). This in turn does little to tackle the real issue of how a valorisation of that difference can in fact enhance your subordinated racialised status in a racist society, as real equality between the 'races' gets placed on the back burner. By celebrating your 'otherness' without addressing the historical circumstances that created that 'otherness' as inferior, you run the risk of becoming embroiled in a series tail chasing exercises. These will serve to further obscure the seminal role you play in your own liberation because, 'the white man has already implanted numerous historical myths in the minds of black peoples; those have to be uprooted' (Rodney, 1969:51).

One way to deploy Rodney's 'uprooting' process is by realising that the right to be different does not equate to a right to be treated as a social, cultural or political equal in this time and place, as this reductive redefinition closes off this prospect by promoting cultural diversity. The problem being that whenever 'we' think of 'cultural diversity' 'we' are mostly thinking about the ways of being of the 'ethnics', those marked as non-white by the dominant white society. The irony is that the whites who are indigenous to the British Isles, especially the English, are seldom described as 'ethnic majorities'. Hence uncritically embracing cultural diversity as the 'right to be different' does little to counter the fact that we are socialised into accepting that 'the whiteness of whiteness is the blindness of wilful innocence' (Lazarre, 1997:49).

Indeed this notion of 'cultural diversity' can, rather ironically, be promoted as 'universally' acceptable, because it does little to dispense with the quaint, exotic, or even bizarre notion of the inferior 'African/black other' that dominates the wider public arena. Similarly, it does not deal with the historical nature of how 'race' and its highly stratified nature has become the norm in contemporary British society. Nor can it explain the manner in which that sense of distance between the 'races' that was formulated and perpetuated by scientific discourse, presently manifests in various acceptable ways of knowing self and other based on a black/white dichotomy. Take for instance the following:

> This fellow was quite black…a clear indication that what he said was stupid…The Negroes of Africa have by nature no

> feelings that rises above the trifling…although many of them have even been set free, still not a single one was ever found who presented anything great in art or science or any other praiseworthy quality. (Kant, cited in Eze, 1997:38/55/56)

Without perhaps considering that:

> They're a people now forgotten discovered while others were yet barbarians, the elements of the arts and sciences. A race of men now rejected for their black skin and woolly hair, founded on the study of the laws of nature those civil and religious systems which still governs the universe. (Volney, cited in Jochannan, 1985:vii)

Now let's be clear, I do not cite the above as an example of waving the black flag and claiming, as many do, that Afrikans created everything and Europeans stole everything; that would be foolish. I cite the above because they allow us to compare the two accounts, both of which were written around the same time by European philosophers. One who suggests that the mere fact that you are 'black' means that you are 'stupid', whilst the other presents a contrast by stating that the people described in this fashion are the ones who 'discovered the arts and sciences' Kant so readily claims is beyond the ken of the 'Negroes of Africa'. The point is that the information is there to challenge simplistic and racist aspersions like Kant's, so my question is why these sources are not made readily available in places of learning by 'educators' who know of their existence? The answer is that their omission is deliberate, maintains the status quo, and justifies the idea that Africans are still the 'child race' on this planet. That means those who know different must challenge the manner in which our presence has been documented by historians/anthropologists/sociologists/ philosophers et al, who for generations have wilfully distorted the Afrikan historical presence in their writings.

Such writings mould and shape the imaginations of generation after generation and more so when they have the kudos of Kant who is often cited as the 'father of Enlightenment philosophy'. The fact other testimonies counter some of the most pernicious commentaries on the Afrikan, during the 'Enlightenment' period, is significant to this argument, and explains why I am compelled to make the Afrikan contribution to world history, pre-chattel enslavement known. This is the best way to challenge these gross misrepresentations, for their exclusion speaks to how the Afrikan personality has been consciously and systematically attacked by racist Europeans for specific reasons. The most obvious being to maintain the illusion that Africa is the 'dark continent' and consequently:

> …an African living in the margins of his or her own history with little knowledge of the traditions that generate our thoughts and behaviour tends to accept as normal what is bizarre and abnormal. What is it to be off-centred? Dislocated?

> Misplaced? It is to be lulled into the belief that you can simultaneously be sane and decentred culturally. (Asante, 1994:3)

The suggestion is that if the mind suffering from the legacy of chattel enslavement is externally controlled, then the actions driven by that mind cannot be analysed by solely looking within. By doing so the power differential in the relations between so called blacks and whites will remain hidden and the 'decentred' African will remain confused. Simply put, white people do not really have to consider how their whiteness is an ever-present non-presence that moulds and shapes a lived reality; which bestows 'gifts', 'benefits' and 'privileges' upon them that have to be 'earned', in one way or another, by black people. We must therefore be aware of how the hierarchical 'distance' that was created between the 'races' during modernity's quest for scientific rationality, has been replaced by a 'distance' created by recognising acceptable difference. Because, 'although white racism affects all "non-white" peoples, Africans and people of African ancestry are the particular targets of the resurgence of a neo-scientistic racism' (Rigby 1996:2/3). A mindset that impacts on our present social reality as exemplified in the work of the 'bell curve' theorists (Herrnstein & Murray 1996) who still hold fast to racist Enlightenment principles.

We may be of a mind to believe that the days of using this type of irrational 'rationality' for explaining human variation is no longer relevant, but it was in 2006 that a university professor in Leeds, who is an advocate of the 'bell curve' theory, suggested that 'on average, black people are less intelligent than white people' (Gabriel 2006). Regardless of how incredibly racist and scientifically untenable we may find such a suggestion, it speaks to the persistence of 'race' as a tool of subjugation. Hence 'once subjectified these bodies could be analysed, categorised, classified, and ordered with the cold gaze of scientific distance (Goldberg cited in Young, 1996:41).

The distance between Europeans and Afrikans has been maintained through a discourse that subsumes the social, cultural and political dimensions of 'subjectless bodies', and subsequently offers solutions that appeal to a common-sense understanding of difference. These appeals to common sense do little to dispel the inherently stratified nature of racial thinking and many theorists, inadvertently, give this viewpoint an assist as they argue for a celebration of the right to be different. Advocating the right to be different has created a tension in sociological thinking, a veritable 'crisis of modernity' as modernist equations of 'reason' with 'freedom' are rejected. Furthermore, modernist forms of rationality are deemed to be 'reductive' and 'oppressive' as they are nothing more than ideological 'constructs of domination' (Best & Kellner, 1991:237) that overlook the seminal role European aggression played in the creation and maintenance of these constructs.

Fanon's writings on such constructs are replete with examples of how the 'plural' nature of 'colonial societies' manifest in real life situations and how 'racial pluralism' determines the rules for both 'oppression' and 'resistance'. It is crucial that we understand this relationship because it helps to explain why the struggles of black communities, economic or otherwise, cannot be reduced to the historical experiences of white communities or individuals. Our right to be different is a necessary consequence of wilful segregation, because if we are honest we know that what often separates 'us' blacks, from 'them' whites, is generally what unites 'them' against 'us'. Consequently, part of the way we arguably socialise ourselves and our children in the 'mother' country, is to realise that living whilst black is a 'problem' in a racist society.

Further, 'racial socialization is the process whereby we come to know our strengths, understand the world in which we live, and position ourselves to strive' (Leary, 2005:200). In attempting to explain why this is so, Fanon states that in the 'colonial' context, the 'cause is the consequence; you are rich because you are white, you are white because you are rich' (Fanon, 1990:31). Following this line of argument, Fanon suggests that because the 'whites' became rich through a 'colonialism' premised on 'violence', the 'moral justification' of 'violence' derives from 'the good fortune of those who rule, and the misery of those who are ruled' (Kuper, 1974:67). Think back to

Blair's comments on black people and the need for 'specific measures [for 'us'] to be brought back into the fold' and you will realise that there is much to what Fanon suggests. In fact 'it seems uncontroversial to claim that the roots of the racialized postmodern city can be traced to the end of the colonial era' (Goldberg, 1995:46).

Goldberg suggests that in order to understand the roots of contemporary forms of social control and exclusion, we must consider how spaces are reconfigured both in the physical and psychological senses in contemporary British society. That is why I mentioned above the importance of acknowledging how and why we have come to 'live' in the places we do in Europe's 'new world'. I am claiming that in order to comprehend the sites of resistance and transcendence that have enabled the black communities to be here in this place and at this time, we need to appreciate the role and purpose of retaining a sense of difference, in a hostile environment. I am suggesting that we must appreciate how certain members of the global Afrikan/black family recognise the commonalty of our condition and use this knowledge as a source of strength and empowerment wherever we happen to dwell in Babylon.

Conclusion

Many who have endeavoured to theorise the impact of white racism on the black communities in the UK have failed to regard this relationship as one of ongoing European aggression against peoples of Afrikan ancestry. Failing to perceive it as such ensures that our immediate concerns have either been viewed through the lens of wider social relations, or have been dismissed entirely as matters of re-education. Such re-education generally entails stripping away the worldviews and cultural forms that the migrants brought with them, along with their suitcases, when they came to these shores as the Windrush generation. In other words what hinders their full assimilation as British citizens is in essence the tried and trusted modes of resistance and transcendence that were a constant source of re-linking with their humanity during the MAAFA. Hence any explanation of contemporary black life must interrogate the critical role that notions of whiteness play in an inherently racist society like Britain. By doing so we will be better placed to unshackle the Afrikan mind and mount a meaningful challenge to white supremacist thought and action, that offers an alternative epistemological and ontological take on what it means to black from an 'insider' perspective.

A failure to do so is to remain complicit in our own self destruction for the mainstay of the black communities have been, and still are, the identifiably black cultural forms that the Windrush generation utilised when they arrived in Britain to ensure theirs and our continued survival. To overlook the significance of the building blocks they left for future generations is to do them and our ancestors a gross injustice. This is what needs to be understood in any endeavour to better our current racialised predicament in meaningful and practical ways. That is why I focused on sociological and other explanations of black behaviour and critically evaluated their role in creating a black object of enquiry that is often rendered voiceless in the analysis. At the same time I offered a corrective by interrogating and unveiling the centrality of whiteness to the black experience in the UK, as a means to provide a meaningful definition of contemporary racism from a 'sociological' perspective.

Witnesses to whiteness: making the invisible, visible

> I believe whiteness is an attitude, mental/spiritual state, that has purpose of function and dominates all nine areas of human activity (nine in numerology meaning completion) this is why Whiteness has become synonymous with being "human." One of the functions and achievements of the Nation of Islam (NOI) was to highlight, expose and effectually make whiteness extremely visible…Not only was the "American dream" flipped as the "American nightmare" but whiteness itself was redefined. Its history and its very purpose of function were given new meaning. **Brother Hakim**

London, United Kingdom, 2004

As part of the annual Black History Month celebrations that take place during the month of October in the UK I am invited by my local councils, Lewisham and Greenwich, to deliver a talk on a theme of my choice on the black experience in the UK. What generally happens is I submit an outline of what I intend to discuss for inclusion in the brochure that would contain the theme as well as the details of the time and venue, and I always insist that these events are free. In 2004, due to what I regarded as an unprecedented, ill informed and unjustified attack on certain Reggae performers, spearheaded by a notorious homosexual activist, I decided to deliver a talk that would challenge the mass censorship and banning that resulted from these attacks. I therefore submitted my outline as normal and below is an account of what happened from that moment on as a way to demonstrate how whiteness works in mundane, everyday situations. It will be followed by an article I wrote on the matter of Black History Month for Black Britain, an online newspaper, in 2005.

OUTRAGE-'US': BOOM BYE BYE TO FREEDOM OF SPEECH! (Submitted 7th July 2004)

> In this talk Dr. Lez Henry will focus on the manner in which ideas of race, gender and sexuality are represented in reggae/dancehall music and consider the validity of the charges of homophobia, that are being used to deny Jamaican artistes the right to perform in front of black communities in Britain. All that is asked is that you bring your mind and make sure it is open. Hotep!

Dear Dr Henry (4th August 2004)

Thank you for your copy for the Black History Month brochure that …has shared with me. Your proposed talk "Outrage US Boom Boom Bye Bye to Freedom of Speech" certainly sounds the basis for a topical and Controversial discussion. I have no doubt that your aim is to hold an objective and balanced debate. I am however concerned that the event could give the opportunity for others to use it to promote views and opinions that might cause offence or conflict in some sections of the community. As such an event of the kind proposed would not fit particularly well with the tone that has been established for Black History Month in Lewisham over many years, we would not wish to fund it as part of the programme for this year.

I hope this decision will not deter you from making further contributions to Black History Month this year and the future.

yours sincerely…
Acting Executive Director of Education & Culture

Dear … (4th august 2004)

I think it is strange that my lecture was pulled without consultation. There has been no dialogue between myself and anyone in a senior position, those who really make the decisions that matter, about the concerns that have been expressed with regards to my proposed talk. Yet the supreme irony is that the way the council have handled the whole affair is exactly why I wanted to have this discussion in the first place. You can state that you are wary about the reactions/actions of 'others' in the community, without stating exactly who these 'others' are, or more importantly what these concerns are. For to suggest that you know my discussion would be 'balanced and objective' and then deny me the opportunity to present it, or even discuss how it could be re-presented so as not to cause 'offence' to whoever it is you are concerned about, is disingenuous and patronising to the extreme.

I think it is insulting and offensive that a community that has a single month allocated to them to redress the imbalances caused by institutionalised racism and other forms of discrimination, that are endemic to this racist society, have faceless gatekeepers telling them, as taxpayers and members of Lewisham Borough, who can speak to them about the issues that affect their everyday existence. You see you cannot expect me to take seriously any claim about conflict, when it is out of conflict that the whole idea of black history month arose, firstly in the USA and then here. Moreover, it would have been respectful to engage in some form of dialogue about what is at stake in the lecture, as in the outline I stated that I was interested in discussing, Race, Gender and Sexuality in reggae music and yet the only problem was my usage of the word 'homophobia'. This means that once again people who do not appreciate the seriousness of these issues, as part of the legacy of colonialism in all of its pernicious manifestations, including much that is suggested in reggae music, have denied those who the music affects the most from having a reasoned and informed debate about what is important to us, the black community in Britain. But I suppose this is freedom of speech, for those who generally react without an in depth knowledge of that which they are reacting to.
Dr. William Henry

Witnesses to whiteness: making the invisible, visible

Reflections on the Black History Season

> Why is it that as Afrikans we are told by Europeans we have no history and yet everywhere you go on the planet you find our artefacts filling museums. The truth is we are the best kept secret on the planet! Anthony Browder (1990, Recorded Lecture)

> The image of the West with which the world has been bombarded is one that has served the purposes of continued European political and cultural/ideological domination. European cultural domination has done a formidable job. Marimba Ani (1994: 570)

> Dem tek weh wi gold and tek wi silver, dem hang mi puppa an rape mi mother, dem tek weh wi name an call wi nigger, the only words we know, I'se ah comin massa, dem tell wi seh wi ignorant an inferior, an how dem intelligent an superior, through the complexion of them skin colour. (Papa Levi, 1983, Ghettotone Sound System)

Greetings.

It pleases me immensely to be given this opportunity to air my thoughts on the significance of Black History Month in the UK. If the truth be told I am 'Christmas crackered' (knackered) by my perennial endeavours to put black back on the historical map, which intensify during this month. In fact it is during moments of reflection like this that I am reminded as to why after being so enthused with the introduction of this month in 1987, I began to avoid it. This was because it bothered me greatly that as an Afrikan I had to seemingly prove to all and sundry that I had a history.

Think of how ludicrous it is to claim that as members of the human family Afrikans have contributed nothing of note to the human experience. Lest you think I exaggerate consider what you are generally told in the mainstream, be it school, college, university or the white/European-dominated media in its myriad manifestations that Afrikans have given to the world. Take away anything that can be regarded as rudimentary cultural expression, i.e. singing, dancing, cooking, etc. and see what's left. Not much I'll wager and that is what needs to be challenged and one month a year is nowhere near enough time to counter over 2000 years of damage and wilful misrepresentation of Afrikan humanity.

I had a change of heart and began to partake in Black History Month a few years ago for one main reason, which was that black history had vanished from that which was introduced to give black people visibility. This meant that the Afrikan presence that is central to 'black history' had in my experience been replaced with 'ethnic' expression. For example I went to an event in the late 1990s and witnessed Irish folk dancers performing as part of a Black History Month celebration and they were very entertaining. Now don't get me wrong as I know that had I been blessed with the ability to read when

I was born, I would have read the signs that English white folk so brazenly put outside their front doors stating No blacks, No Irish, No dogs.

I also know that until fairly recently the Irish were still known as the 'niggers of Europe', but I still couldn't understand why they were featured in a month that was supposedly designed to address the concerns of non-white people in general and Afrikans in particular. For like it or not, those who introduced this month to the British Isles did so for this reason, yet due to the confusion around what it means to be black the term has become one of convenience for any group that believe they are oppressed.

Unsurprisingly then, I was charged with being unrealistic and separatist at a black conference, earlier this year, by a few black scholars who suggested that black should be all inclusive. Hence my usage of BLAK to signify those of us who recognise that as Afrikans our problems with racist Europeans are historically different from other 'black' groups. Pointing out that Africans were reduced to 3/5ths human or 'articles of commerce', the only members of the human family to be reduced to a mathematical equation, did not go down well with them. Things got even worse when I pointed out to them that as chattel slaves we were bought, sold, used, abused, bred, and traded like any other beast of burden the white god gave Europeans dominion over.

I then suggested they perhaps need to appreciate that slavery in ancient Greece was like being a child in a nursery compared to the chattel enslavement of Africans and as such they need to be mindful of historical differences. To make the point clearer and without intentionally throwing more fuel on the racial fire that currently burns in the Lozell's area in Birmingham, how are the main protagonists identified? Is it not as black and Asian? This makes little sense when 'black' as the only negation of 'white' is a political construct and Asia is a geographical region, a continent (or so we are told but look at a map and tell me where Europe ends and Asia begins)? There is something radically wrong with this picture that I cannot deal with in this short piece, but suffice to say that someone is playing the non-white communities in Britain like a grand piano and it is sometimes dangerous to dance to a tune you did not write for yourself.

This said it was to do my best to combat this form of confusion that I began to give public speeches, talks, lectures and seminars, in other words to put myself about as much as possible and join my brothers and sisters who are determined to make our story known, wherever we happen to live on this planet. That is why I opened this piece with three quotes that speak to our global condition as Afrikans on the receiving end of global white supremacist thought and action, in the Motherland and throughout the Diaspora. Browder speaks to the confusion that reigns in the teaching of so called 'black history', when as Afrikans we are regularly informed by Eurocentric scholars, both black and white that we have no history of note.

Yet the oldest forms of written documentation and historical artefacts that inform the world of the breadth, depth and significance of the Afrikan contribution to the human experience are locked away behind plate glass in European museums. Imagine how preposterous it is to witness how grave robbers like Howard Carter are celebrated for stealing Afrikan artefacts, yet the creators of the artefacts are held in global contempt. As Papa Levi suggested "dem tek weh wi name an call wi nigger", in other words Europeans rape the people and the continent, rob the people of their knowledge of self and then blame them for their condition, which is grounded in the whitening of the black contribution to world history from Nubia to Benin and beyond.

I was subjecting myself to BBC news recently and saw a plug for a new programme that features Carter's 'discovery' of Tut-ankh-Amen's (break up the name and it makes more sense) tomb. In the bulletin a white female Egyptologist, stated that it was Napoleon who first 'discovered' Ancient Kemet/Egypt. However what she failed to share with the knowing public was that upon seeing the face of the Sphinx, Napoleon allegedly aimed his canons and fired upon it in an effort to rearrange its 'negroid' facial features.

This may sound far fetched but have you noticed how many of the artefacts that were stolen from this part of Afrika have no noses or lips, yet everything else remains intact? Moreover, it is widely stated that the face of the sphinx was that of Khafre, although according to one of the most knowledgeable Afrikan scholars I know, Rey Bowen: "The face is definitely pre-dynastic and as such far older than many would have us believe."

Either way its face bore no resemblance to Napoleon what so ever and because this is the case then we need to think about how 'black history' is whitened, repackaged and used as a tool against us. That is why Marimba Ani quite rightly argues that "European cultural domination has done a formidable job" on us as Afrikans by bombarding us during our every living and breathing moments, with all things white and beautiful. If this is the case, then how can we as Afrikans, seriously expect to take one month out of the year to right this blatant and ongoing wrong?

My suggestion is that Black History Month must be used as another weapon in our arsenal to fight against the constant and blatant action that misrepresents the Afrikan humanity with impunity. This means that as Afrikans we must realise that wherever we are in the Diaspora or in Afrika itself the struggle must be ongoing, as the world we have inherited does not ease up, which means nor should we. I am not for one moment suggesting that we are all the same and have the same experiences because we clearly do not. Rather I am suggesting that the hour is late and we can no longer delude ourselves that things are getting better, because how can we idly sit back and accept a global system that was not designed to benefit the majority of the people on this planet, much less the Afrikan? W. Henry (www.blackbritain.co.uk, 31/10/2005)

> Whiteness is a social construct created by the group who have cloaked themselves in this identity to forge group identity and loyalty and as a catalyst for their ongoing psychopathic, racially motivated wars of imperialism. Whiteness has been constructed as the superior antithesis of 'Blackness' which it seeks to degrade. Whiteness sucks Afrikans into an identity based upon colour/pigment alone and seeks to divert us from the platform of Land, History and Culture upon which Afrikaness - the best antidote to Whiteness for us - rests. **Paul Ifayomi Grant**

> We African diasporan scholars have to give whiteness a 'black eye' - thoroughly interrogate it to reveal how, despite its instability, it functions as a place of privilege. **Dr. Robert Beckford**

Too black for your own good: Head-Decay-Shun

Introduction

> At school the teachers taught me things like how to use a lathe, couldah ask them any question bout when man live innah cave, if me ask them bout when blackman down innah slave, them blush, turn red, them answer used to scathe, I'll give you an example of the answer they gave, bloody trouble maker, get out the class, until you learn to behave. (Lezlee Lyrix 1983)

> My mind is the place I make my plan, the world is the place I take my stand! (Dead Prez, Psychology, 2000)

What does it mean when you are accused of being 'too black for your own good'? A charge that has been levelled against me from the moment I began 'public' speaking as a Reggae dancehall deejay over twenty five years ago. In my experiences I have found that what people generally mean is 'you know too much', 'you think too much', 'you question too much', 'you read into things too much', you challenge too much', 'you read until you turn fool', all because I dare to seek an alternative knowledge of self. For this reason I want us to consider what it means to educate in concordance with educere, the Latin word for to 'draw out and develop' what resides within, as my experiences of a compulsory Head-Decay-Shun in a racist society were more often to the contrary. I want 'educators' in particular, to therefore think through the relationship between schooling (as training) and education as that which engenders an ongoing and more complete understanding of a society's dominant culture, socially, economically and politically. The type of ongoing edification that one would consider crucial to a more grounded understanding of how a society works and therefore how one can successfully navigate a sane path through it.

In the context of the contemporary, black/Afrikan children need to understand this form of social navigation and therefore need to be educated about a positive self when dwelling/learning in a society where whiteness is valued and blackness is not. Why? Well in British society they do not receive anything of note from the National Curriculum about a thinking black/Afrikan historical self that is positive and uplifting and not reliant on a history that begins, and more or less ends, with chattel enslavement. By the way this is wilful and deliberate for, as Paul Obinna has been pointing out for years, the reality is that:

> The British Schools and National Curriculum offers valuable guidelines for any community groups wishing to see positive content inputs in relation to knowledge that helps to raise Black children's self-esteem. The second paragraph of the

Curriculum's 'Values, Aims & Purposes' opens with the statement:

> 'Foremost is a belief in education, at home and at school, as a route to the spiritual, moral, social, cultural, physical and mental development, and thus the well-being, of the individual'. Under the Aims, the statement continues that:
>
> 'If schools are to respond effectively to these values and purposes, they need to work in collaboration with family-lies and the local community, including church and voluntary groups, local agencies and business, in seeking to achieve two broad aims through the curriculum'. These aims provide an essential context within which schools develop their own curriculum. (Obinna, 2007)

I believe that once black educators need to use the spaces where a positive notion of the Afrikan can be introduced to our young people before they totally self-destruct. They need to be encouraged to 'belong' to something other than 'English' (in all its manifestations) that is not chided by some derider who does not appreciate how we use Afrikan culture for self-empowerment. One way to do so that in my experience is accessible and overly effective, is to provide a space where they can use their perspective as a starting point. This is achieved by exploring alternative ways of knowing, being, experiencing, and writing about the relationship between black people and white society that at least opens the door to other possible forms of black identification.

Equally I want to convey how it is possible to derive a sense of self-worth that is based on being 'self'-educated—premised upon an Afrikan-centred-self—as opposed to being educated away from 'self', which is what happens to many of us in schools, colleges and universities. I will argue that we need to experience a form teaching where the learning is not constrained by the boundaries of the English language, the effects of which will be positively uplifting and socially empowering.

Written out of reality: black Objects of exclusion

> Many people have labelled me a racist, cos I express my feelings in front of their faces, ask me what it's like to be born and raised in this country, first thing I'll tell you is for us it ain't easy. One of my first memories as a kid, was the kind of statement that left me livid, like adult whites who you think would know better, living out the colonial mind to the letter, teaching their kith and kin that anything with a blak skin, is the product of sin, nothing better than a two legged mule, the Hollywood fool only fit for ridicule, at school their kids would ask me questions like these; have I got a tail do I swing in trees, is my head full of lice am I riddled with disease, my dad said you're a dog do you harbour fleas? My fist would answer questions like these, but as I matured and got to realise,

> these were the savages and I was civilized, how could they tell me that I was ignorant, then call me a monkey's uncle as a serious statement, we've caused some abatement to this way of thinking, from the fountain of blackness the whole world is drinking, look at our music our style our culture, embraced by the youth the whole world over, so never complain or show any shame, if anyone ever tells you, you're too blak in Brixtain. (Lezlee Lyrix, Too Blak In Brixtain, 1989)

One day in the spring of 1989, after yet another argument with a potential mainstream record producer about my lyricism's uncompromising, Africentric stance, I composed the lyric from which the above verse is drawn. In fact I featured the full track on the demo tape I would send to potential producers so there was no confusion about who they were dealing with and what my perspective was (yes you 'young uns' back in the day it was not the CD way we have today). Yet although I had several meetings not one record company offered me an album deal, which was unsurprising as they knew I will never compromise my beliefs for anyone, much less to those who seek to, as Immortal Technique suggests, 'control perspective'. Crucially in the lyric I argue that as a person born and raised in South east London, England, my lived experience of racism has been a part of my reality for as long as I can remember. The reason for this is obvious when we consider that for many black people who attempt to think through our condition, individually or collectively in a whitened world, the realization soon dawns upon us that we are still battling the 'ongoing project of African dehumanization' (Tate, 1992: 244).

Further, I argue in the lyrical extract above that once you dare to speak, or write, frankly about what it means to be black in a white world, you are invariably labelled as being 'too black' 'a racist, 'a racist in reverse' or 'black supremacist'. I think I need to point out here that 'Too Blak In Brixtain' was written four years before I returned to full-time education as a mature student, which means that my concerns then and now reflect my lived (not academically abstracted) experiences. Experiences that cannot be fixed or rooted in one geographical region, which was the logic behind my playing with the words Britain and Brixton to create a more meaningful term to describe the homogenising of a lived black reality. A reality that to this day remains relatively hidden along the ebbs and flows of Gilroy's 'Black Atlantic', which is why we must educate the world about our experiences of white domination. This will enable those of Afrikan ancestry to recognise the commonality of our condition and use this knowledge to fight a unified battle for social justice on a global level.

I noticed that when I first went to the USA in 1985, many of the African-Americans or Afrikans in America I reasoned with would immediately 'tell me' that I lived in Brixton. In such cases, often due to their exposure to Brixton's various uprisings via American TV, there was amazement when I informed them that Brixton is just one place that blacks inhabit in London, not to mention the rest of the United Kingdom. Therefore, the grasping of an alternative written reality that links supposedly disparate elements from across the Afrikan Diaspora, such as the African-American/black 'Hollywood fool' (captured par excellence by Public Enemy in the video of their single 'Burn Hollywood Burn') with the story of a black man born in Britain who experiences the same ridiculous, dehumanising treatment, requires much consideration. The point is blacks in Britain and obviously in many other colonised spaces and places, from day one, are bombarded with negative representations that directly impact on their performance in the educational arena. For instance, consider the following slice of reasoning that came out of some sessions I taught on the Afrikan/ black presence in world history.

The sessions were delivered in July/August 2003 to several, predominantly black, year 11 students (approx 16 years old) as part of a 'Gifted and Talented' 2003 Summer School program. The students were all stumped when one day I asked them the following question. Name me something/anything positive you have learned about people of Afrikan ancestry/black people, in school, and you can't mention Rosa Parks, Nelson Mandela or Dr Martin Luther King? What transpired was memorable as it was the quietest these students had been in any of the sessions and the silence lasted for about a minute or two. I broke the ice by stating that they should not 'feel ah way' about not knowing/learning about Afrikan history in British schools, because this is invariably the response I receive from their peers when asked the same question. I suggested to them that as a community we all, adults and children, need to think seriously about what is happening in the places we are supposedly sending them, our children, to learn. This is the moment when I invited them to consider the following that perhaps allows us to think through why this is so important because firstly as Marcus Garvey argued:

> The great white man has succeeded in subduing the world by forcing everyone to think his way, from his God to his fireside. He has given to the world, from his bible to his yellow newspaper sheet, a literature that establishes his right and sovereignty to the disadvantage of the rest of the human race. (Garvey, cited in Martin 1986:89)

Before I carry on I need to draw something to your attention. I think it is scandalous that on many occasions when I teach, at all levels, hardly any of the students have heard of Marcus Garvey. In this instance out of 17 students only 4 had learned about the works of Marcus Garvey and this was from their parents or family members. This is significant because of the predominance of the Afrikan-Caribbean community in Britain and is a damning indictment on how we must do better as communities to educate ourselves and our young people on such a crucial champion of pan-Afrikan liberation. This said Garvey eloquently posits that we must challenge the manifestations of whiteness if we are to make the significant changes that will guarantee our collective future. Especially when considering what happens to the black child in that classroom situation where 'someone with the authority of a teacher say describes the world and you are not in it, there is a moment of psychic disequilibrium as if you looked into a mirror and saw nothing' (Riche, cited in Rosaldo 1989:xi).

Not seeing yourself in what you are being taught in a racist society means you become an object of exclusion, which is part of the strategy a dominant culture uses to perpetuate your inferiority as a negative racial other, to their positive racial self. That is why 'educators' must focus on rigorously challenging and altering the culture of learning, encouraging our young people to strive for educational excellence within the constraints of this system. For as Coard suggested over three decades ago it is the duty of black educators to make known that:

> Black history and culture, i.e. the history of Black people throughout the Caribbean, the Americas, Africa and Asia, should be made a part of the curriculum of all schools, for the benefit of the Black and white children...Indeed its exclusion from most school curricula constitutes nothing short of criminal negligence (or prejudice) in the educational sphere. (Coard 1991:44)

Too black for your own good: Head-Decay-Shun

I then suggested to the students that the above, when taken together, more or less explains my experiences of the educational system in Britain over thirty years ago, during the moment when Coard's (1971) seminal work on 'black underachievement' was first published. I, like many of them, was born and raised in London as part of a large family by parents who hailed from beyond these shores, in my case they came from Jamaica to Britain in the early 1950s. My parents thought it was essential for their children to respect themselves as black people and take full advantage of an educational system, touted as the best in the world. They firmly believed that education was the best racial and social equalizer and that once 'educated' properly, one could compete with anyone, irrespective of race, colour, or creed. At this time they were unaware of the fact that there was a 'hidden curriculum… and…even the best of teachers cannot protect his pupils from it' (Illich, 1971:32). This obviously is based on inculcating and reinforcing the racist and social stereotypes, prevalent in all aspects of British society, then and now.

Moreover, as I point out all of the time, the 1944 Education Act introduced the tripartite system that we inherited as a consequence of our parents coming here, during the fifties and sixties and it was not designed for our benefit. It was designed to maintain the deep class divisions that are the bane of this society and consequently we got lumped in with the white working class children who were schooled for failure. The reality is that in Britain, as in many other societies, some are 'destined' for manual work, some to work in offices and some inevitably to rule. My parents can be excused for their optimism as they had not been in Britain very long and had never experienced this particular educational system. A system which was based on a notion of creating a 'new Jerusalem' (city of peace) on the back of the post 1939-45 war optimism, by offering an 'education for all' based on merit and equality.

My parents were soon to learn that far from being based on some form of meritocracy, the educational system ensured that the distribution of education was geared towards the maintenance of the status quo. This disorients the Afrikan/black child by encouraging them to accept as 'truth' the negative association of themselves as the inferior black other, to a white positive self, as a natural aspect of everyday life. Often they get locked into what Carby (1999:189) dubs 'the cycle of pathology'. A consequence of many black youth being forcibly socialized into a culture of social practices that do not reflect the differences in the reality of their relationship to life in British society, because:

> Those who control the state schooling systems in Britain and the United States are not about to alter the misinformation

> inculcated through their schools. Schooling of this kind is needed to reinforce the cultural values and beliefs that maintain the existing power relations. These cultural values and beliefs have historically undermined the integrity and dignity of Africans while at the same time justifying African oppression. (Dove 1994:344)

The crucial point is that those who came to Britain, during the same moment as my parents, had more than enough problems to contend with in an openly hostile and racist society. Seeking employment or finding suitable accommodation was a veritable nightmare for many, and thus they often entrusted our learning to the state's various institutions. Unsurprisingly with encouraging words in our ears and a will to succeed, my parents' children were sent one by one, or in the case of my twin brother and I, by two into the school environment.

The first real eye opener I had into the racist exclusionary practice that masquerades as an impartial educational system that did not, would not, and could not cater for the needs of an Afrikan child, occurred when my brother and I were preparing to leave primary school. We were 11 years old and thus legally obliged to begin our secondary education. We had both qualified academically to be considered for a place at our local Grammar School (Brockley County). However, our Headmistress who shall eternally remain nameless in 'my book', in her infinite wisdom convinced our parents that the local comprehensive school was far more 'suitable' for 'us' at this time. The nickname for the school we ended up in sufficiently reveals her ulterior motive, methinks, as it was called Samuel 'Sambo' Pepys because of the high percentage of black pupils who were sentenced to go there. This school was in essence a dumping ground for potential social 'no-hopers', therefore many white working class and all the Afrikan/black children more or less fitted this criterion, especially if they spoke with a noticeable accent. Hence those that recently arrived from Afrika, the Caribbean and parts of Southeast Asia would invariably be placed in the lowest classes.

Ironically for those of us who were born here our local ac-cent at least ensured that we had a chance of being placed in the higher classes and this was the case with my brother and I. Always in the top class and yet still treated with contempt by many of our teachers. For example the time when the school librarian called a couple of my black friends and I 'savages and cannibals' because we were, in his opinion, making too much noise in the corridor whilst walking past the library. Let's pause and consider the supreme irony of this situation. The library is the central point of knowledge in the learning environment, yet it was entrusted to a psychopath who would openly spit racist abuse at his charges with impunity. I remember that just like on many other occasions when I challenged such racism, I was treated like an infant (no voice) and invariably ended up being punished by those who had the power to undermine our capacity to 'think' for ourselves.

Similarly I remember going to a secondary school on behalf of one of my sons a few years ago and tackling a teacher who whilst chastising him—for what turned out to be a problem not of his making—used a word, recalcitrant, which he did not understand. When he asked her what it meant she suggested that his not knowing was a mark of his inferiority, which is a clear example of how this educational space was dominated by the teacher's power to include or exclude both formally and informally. I won't dwell on what I said to her but I introduced her to the GREY zone where her whiteness couldn't protect her. At first she 'huffed and puffed', and when she realised that 'me noh easy', she flushed and blushed and climbed down off her high horse. I simply explained to her that she is there to 'educate' and not intimidate or demoralise my thirteen-year-old child. I made her apologise to my son, reminded her of her role as an 'educator' and suggested that in the future she conducts herself in an appropriate fashion or, like Arnie, 'I'll be back'!

Another example of how this power to include or exclude manifests in the school environment, I vividly remember, was an incident that occurred when I was 15 years old. We were having the works of Wilfred Owen rammed down our throats in an English literature class and being constantly reminded of how wonderful he was for writing such profound poetry at such a 'young' age. I believe he was around 24 years old when he wrote 'Anthem for Doomed Youth' which depicted the horrors of the 1914-18 war. We were then instructed to write something original on this theme and when I submitted my poem (probably a week later) I learned a vital new word and something that is very important for all of us, especially those who enter the world of academia, the meaning of plagiarism for that is what they accused me of. However, when several members of staff were consulted and none could find the source I supposedly stole from, I was commended for my literary prowess and rewarded at 'Prize Day' with a book token. A token gesture which they perhaps—that is if they ever considered my feeling—believed would repair the psychological damage inflicted upon me by their false and unfounded allegations.

I did not understand these accusations at the time as I did what came naturally to me which was to write, openly and honestly, about how I felt based on what I knew, or even what I thought I knew, at that given point in my life. However, with quite a few years experience of this type of treatment under my belt, hindsight is a fine thing, I am in a position to share my perspective with others. I fully understand that the teachers had difficulty in coming to terms with the fact that Afrikans can think for themselves, as can any other sentient being. Their real problem was that they, in much the same way as many of us, were the products of a formal education that does not encourage you to think away from Europe as the centre of the universe, intellectually and otherwise. This means they were in my view blissfully unaware that they too were 'educated' in a world where the Afrikan contribution to anything of note was written out of their reality. That is why we are constantly bombarded with 'the first black to achieve this' in much the same way you can take out black and insert African. This mindset only works because the language and physical spaces of formal education, which determines much of our 'intellectual' socialization, are essentially anti the thinking Afrikan.

Moreover, having this knowledge ensures that when I do face overt acts of racial discrimination, I don't break down and cry because my romanticised view of an integrated world has been shattered by certain incidents. For instance, when me and another black student were inside the Sociology Department building, Goldsmiths College, queuing with other students awaiting a tutorial in 1997, a white woman ignored all the other students, who were white, and asked us, the two blacks, if she could help? We just looked at each other, and I said to her 'only if you can get the student out of our tutor's office, so we can get in'. To which the woman turned red and scurried off. Discussing the incident afterwards we put it down to his one and a-half gold teeth and my dreadlocks, as it could not have been our skin colour that was the key factor that drove her offer of assistance, could it? Truth is, in her white-mind we obviously did not 'belong' in that space, making it unreasonable to expect 'blacks' to legitimately have the four digit, door code that was then required to access that building.

Similarly, I remember a few years later when as a lecturer in the said department, I had just left my office when a young white guy asked me if I had any 'skins'? These are the papers one requires to 'roll a joint', 'build-up ah spliff', or whatever you call the preparatory process for smoking Marijuana. I remember politely telling him I did not and I was tempted to show him my name on the office door but realised that it would have made no difference. For him the last thing I could have been was a tutor in the department, which is why I asked a couple of my white male colleagues if this had ever happened to them and it never had. Later on that day I used the experience in a seminar with my students as an example of how racist socialisation works. I obviously fit the stereotype, black man with dread lox; dread lox are Rasta's; Rasta's smoke weed! This takes on a serious dimension when people in positions of power have the ability to enforce their will on those who 'fit' such stereotypes, therefore 'we' must be aware that:

> Since there had been no cultural transformation that enabled white folks to divest of white supremacist thinking, black

> folks were allowed to enter a previously segregated world that appeared to be less racist, even though there had been no critical shift in the racist mindset. (hooks, 1995:242)

Interestingly, hooks makes known that there needs to be a 'critical shift in the racist mindset', thereby endorsing my general point that whiteness works by reducing 'black folks' to the inter-changeable 'other' of the white racist imagination. So merely being non-white in appearance is only part of the explanation of continued black oppression, it is in essence never being able to measure up to white norms that must be acknowledged. For this reason 'the fact that I am writing to you in English already falsifies what I wanted to tell you. My subject: how to explain to you that I don't belong to English though I belong nowhere else' (Firmat, cited in Diaz Junot, 1996). The idea that I 'don't belong to English' yet 'belong nowhere else' sums up how I felt about being accused of plagiarism as a black youth, and why it is important to remember, as Garvey suggested, that 'to see and know your enemy is part of the complete education of man' (cited in Henry, 1996:18). A statement that demonstrates why the recipients of institutionalised racism, must look beyond what is deemed to be a formal, state controlled, 'education'. It is therefore crucial that black 'educators' present information that can be utilized in our common quest for mental liberation.

Moreover when I am reasoning with black youths I select information that they and I can relate to, for instance some of the negative portrayals of black youths in the 1970s – 1980s to show them little has changed. They soon realise why there is still a low expectation placed on them in formal schooling and use the rappers 'Dead Prez' to explain why 'observation and participation, my greatest teachers, when they beat us in our heads with them books they don't reach us' (They Schools, 2000). I am claiming that those who recognize what is truly at stake realise that without these alternatives I doubt if 'we' would have made it this far with 'our' minds intact.

Re-writing reality: Tales of transcendence

In light of my educational experiences one should not be surprised to learn that at 15 years old I sought an alternative education from an Afrikan centre. Under the guidance of one of my older sisters, Christine Asher, who is Rastafari and was 18 years old at the time, I found it in 'Black Studies' at the Moonshot Youth Club, Deptford, South east London, in the early 1970s. I can still recall how uplifted I felt when the tutors, including Ras Cosmo Ben Imhotep, encouraged an Afrikan orientation where to be educated was different from what we experienced in a Eurocentric schooling environment. That which, Rastafari teaches us is in essence 'head-decay-shun', based on an over exposure to that what we encounter in the 'lie-bury'. This means that Rastafari has evaluated the notion of what it is to be 'educated' by your 'enemy', Babylon, and concluded that what occurs is decadent and something to be shunned. Unless of course you appreciate its role in perpetuating Afrikan inferiority and realise 'Man must use Men language to carry dis message' (Bongo Jerry cited in Brathwaite, 1984:37).

Notice how the idea of Rasta as 'Man' and Babylon (the enemy) as 'Men' is crucial to my argument, because it is based on how to think of an alternative self within the confines of the English language. In this sense 'Man' is a metaphor for an enlightened Afrikan humanity which overstands why 'Men' as the agents of Babylon shitstem, continually downpress us in the white world. In much the same way it allows us to appreciate how much of an epistemological problem cultural interpretation can become, when 'you don't belong to English'. A point that is exceptionally well captured by the rappers Dead Prez, whose Africentric perspective on what it is to be 'educated' mirrors my own views on this matter. In fact the tale behind my introduction to the lyricism of 'Dead Prez' best demonstrates how this alternative form of education works. A close friend of mine called me one evening, a few years ago, and informed me that on their album they had a track about schooling, which reminded him of a lyric I used to chat on Sound Systems during the 1980s entitled 'Just be Cool', in which I argued:

> Mi ah goh tell you one story, Rasta know it ah the truth, tell you Lezlee Lyrix was ah conscious youth, five days ah week me mama send me go ah school, when me reach is like the teacher waan fi tek me fool, tell me white man this an them seh white man that, me ask them if black man ah eediot, when them hear that them used to put me ah the back, an den them used to wonder why me never stop chat, den them tell me seh me have too much lip, how pon them shoulder ever Blackman have ah chip, me tell one if me have one there that's where you put-it, he said 'you saucy little git' an give me ears two clip.
>
> Mi tell me mama she seh cool, son stick by the rule, the best years of yuh life is when you learning in school.
>
> When me innah class an them ah chat bout invention, me used to ask them why the Blackman nuh mention, them get vex like I ah cause contention, den them seh Henry two hours detention, ah tell me seh me insolent another one ah seh me impertinent, all because me never feel content, fi sit likah fool an accept them argument. (Lezlee Lyrix, Just Be Cool, 1985)

In the extract, which I use in my sessions with young people, I point out that you are supposedly in school to learn, yet if you ask the 'wrong' type of questions you risk exclusion. I remember arguing with my teachers and telling them that I will never accept that black people never achieved anything. I did not have the knowl-edge/evidence to back up my claims, but just knew something was radically wrong because I recognised that I was cleverer than most of my fellow pupils. I would consistently, academically, outperform the white students who were in the top classes with my brother and I and I knew that I could not be the first Afrikan who has done so. Such knowledge made me realise that what was being done to me and other black people in the classroom was the deliberate ploy of an enemy system that seeks to keep us at the bottom of society. That is why from the day I met this particular person and he realized that I was the deejay Lezlee Lyrix, he told me that it was my lyric about what it means to be 'educated' by your enemy that encouraged him to 'fix-up' and 'educate' himself. As a consequence of this, and the will of the Creator, we ended up on the same degree course at university. In his opinion the Dead Prez track showed that 'nothing has changed in the way black children are taught as they are being fed the same Eurocentric crap as we were where whiteness becomes rightness' (Daniel, Personal Communication, 2000). Hence:

> Why haven't you learned anything? That School shit is a joke, the same people who control the school system control the prison system, and the whole social system, ever since slavery, know what I'm saying…git your lessons that's what my

> moms kept stressing, I tried to pay attention but their classes weren't interesting, they seemed to only glorify the Europeans, claiming Afrikans were only 3/5ths of human beings.
>
> They schools can't teach us shit, my people need freedom we need all we can git, all my high school teachers can suck my dick, telling me white man lies, straight bullshit. They schools ain't teaching us, what we need to know to survive, they schools don't educate, all they teach the people is lies.
>
> School is like a twelve-step brainwash camp, make you think if you drop out you ain't got a chance to advance in life, they make you pull your pants up, students fight the teachers and got took away in handcuffs, and if that wasn't enuff then they expel yah, your folks understand it but to them you're a failure, observation and participation, my greatest teachers, when they beat us in our heads with them books they don't reach us. (Dead Prez, They Schools, 2000)

The reasoning behind Dead Prez's lyric and my own makes known that what we experience is nothing short of being exposed to a process of 'brainwashing' (head-decay-shun), based on Afrikan inferiority. Designed for one main purpose which is to 'glorify the Europeans', whilst concealing the fact that their 'glory' was derived from the brutal subjugation of enslaved Africans, who became the 'natural' antithesis of the white European master. Equally Dead Prez make known that Afrikan chattel enslavement was unlike any other form of un-freedom as we were regarded as '3/5ths human'. Thus the type of 'education' these 'partial humans' received hinged on placing the master, through everyday discourse, at the centre of all things and thus anything that could link the chattel slaves to the Afrikan Continent was brutally suppressed. Especially with regards to the outlawing of the usage of Afrikan languages, as the racist Europeans knew that this was the main conduit for cultural transmission across time and space.

Yet because cultural forms, especially linguistic ones, are far from static and unchanging the recipients of extreme brutality used massas tools, in this case the English language, to dismantle massas worldview. That is how Dead Prez fight against the 'miseducation of the negro' and recognise that 'your folks' will under-stand why 'they schools can't teach us shit'. More importantly, these countercultures present ways to undo the brainwashing process that are pragmatic and practical based on what we have learned about our mutual enemy because:

> The standard GCSE modern world history textbook has chapter after chapter on the world wars, the cold war, British and American life, Stalin's terror and the monstrosities of Nazism - but scarcely a word on the British and other Euro-pean empires which carved up most of the world between them, or the horrors they perpetrated. (Milne, 2005)

Therefore we must, as peoples of Afrikan ancestry realise that 'the true history of a people can only be written and taught by their own knowledgeable scribes and teachers' (Ben-Jochannan, cited in Henry 1996:18). Fundamentally then, I am not talking about the necessity for outer displays of Africanisms, which suggest that to be 'African' one has to dress, speak, eat or think in a particular way. Rather I am thinking about acknowledging a commonality of our condition in Afrika and throughout the Diaspora, and pooling our resources to reclaim the power to define our own 'reality'. However, to reach this point you must be aware that there are alternative ways of thinking yourself into being because the physically brutal master-chattel slave relationship is no longer required to control the 'inferior African'. Many minds are still shackled by those white supremacists who through their global domination of the mainstream media, control, mould and shape, 'reality', which is why Patterson suggests we need to consider:

> The ease with which it is to shift from the meaning of "master" as "man having control or authority" to that of "a teacher or one qualified to teach" reflects the ease with which it is possible to shift from our conception of the slave plantation as a brutal system of exploitation and human degradation to a pastoral college for the edification of poor savages eager to learn the superior arts of the civilized "master". (1982:334/5)

Too black for your own good: Head-Decay-Shun

Afrikan people must recognise that our enemy is not going to relinquish the grasp they have on our minds by offering viable solutions to the problems they created for us in the first place. Rather they will present history in a shroud of whiteness where the 'savage European master' became the 'civilised master' of African 'savages'. And why shouldn't they when they make it plain that their world is based not only on 'the survival of the fittest', but also the survival of the richest. Hence we Afrikans must document and disseminate our own stories by 'any means necessary', as Minister Malcolm X told us, so that our tales of transcendence can be used to empower those yet to come in our tactical battles against global, white domination. For as Hurston reminds us:

> The theory behind our tactics: "The white man is always trying to know into somebody else's business. All right, I'll set him something outside the door of my mind for him to play with and handle. He can read my writing but sho' can't read my mind. I'll put this play toy in his hand, and he will seize it and go away. Then I'll say my say and sing my song." (Hurston, cited in Dundes 1990:iv)

Knowing when to open and close the 'door' to the 'mind' was how the oppressed passed on these types of knowledge, our own 'business' to future generations, ensuring that the culture/language/people would survive racial genocide at the hands of racist Europeans.

Confronting this reality meant the Afrikan mind-space became the ultimate survival kit for this is where 'saying my say and singing my song', becomes crucial to our re-education within the counter cultural confines of the Afrikan Diaspora.

Conclusion

I believe it is prudent for the scholar/educator of Afrikan ancestry to make known how a commonality of condition needs to be distinguished from the homogenization of the black experience, as evidenced in much Eurocentric dogma that masquerades as 'objective' teaching. This means the notion of being a black scholar, located in the UK, needs to explained/interrogated from an Afrikan-centred perspective that seeks to establish a more culturally, spiritually and psychologically relevant approach to solving 'our' problems with the way we are constantly misrepresented. The types of problems many of us face by virtue of our skin colour alone and that plain and simple truth must not be forgotten. More so when the wilful, racist, media distortions and the abstracted academic enterprise, that fails to draw on the narratives of real people becomes the 'acceptable' way of 'knowing' all there is to know about the experiences of black folk.

Simply put, I am the one who is taking 'licks', but someone else has to tell me what the 'licks' feel like, which for me is objectivity gone mad. My lived experiences of being on the receiving end of racism, as detailed above, are of no merit to those who obviously are in the position to 'know' all there is to 'know' about my existence. This attitude to the representation of a lived experience, that I believe is a crucial tool in our quests for a more complete education, really bothers me and has bothered me before and since my return to the educational arena. A situation that becomes more and more trying as I have a hard time seeing myself as an Afrikan in a positive light in much that I read, and am expected to objectively teach/educate from. Never more so than when students of all races, ages and abilities, ask me the types of questions that would not be too difficult to answer if the information was made readily available to them. In such cases I have to point them in the direction of the reasonings of various Afrikan-centred scholars, whose works are perhaps 'Too Black' to be found in the lie-bury.

Witnesses to whiteness: making the invisible, visible

> Whiteness = the manipulated triangulation of political, economic, social and cultural capital whose focus is to dilute the concentration of any other colour. **Sireita Mullings**

Of royals, gaffes and old colonials

> Prince Harry stunned partygoers by attending a pal's birthday bash dressed as a Nazi soldier. Harry, 20, wore the swastika and desert uniform of Rommel's hated German Afrika Korps to the party in West Littleton, Wilts. Last night he said: "I am very sorry if I have caused any offence. It was a poor choice of costume and I apologise." (www.thesun.co.uk/article)

It's ironic that the furore surrounding Prince Harry's latest indiscretion has caused such outrage, in not only the Jewish, but also it seems in the wider global, generally white, communities? All of the old clichéd excuses are being reeled out for and against and to be honest, I don't have time for them here. What is of interest to me is the matter of the context in which he displayed his ill taste. After all it was a fancy dress party, which to most people is reason enough to dress-up, in costume, for a bit of a laugh. That is unless you are the poor soul who dared to dress-up as Osamah Bin Laden a couple of years ago and was subjected to some 'steady licks' (and not with the tongue like our Harry's experiencing), from amongst others, one individual who was dressed as Satan Himself.

I remember reading this at the time and thought what the hell (pardon the pun) is wrong with these people? Do they not possess a sense of humour for if anyone should be beaten it should be the Devil? That's when I thought that humour like most other cultural artefacts is mediated through acceptable and unacceptable forms of behaviour, that are often determined from without by those who have the power to do so. In other words those who are in positions to determine what is important enough, historically, to be commemorated also determine what is overlooked, safely forgotten, and therefore open to ridicule. I am yet to hear one single soul question the theme of the party that gave rise to Harry's little jape, which was an 'old colonials and natives party'. For this reason let's, as we say in Jamaica 'stick ah pin' and consider what is really at stake in this picture with regards to historical memory.

As an Afrikan it saddens me that my holocaust is seldom acknowledged, much less the impact that centuries of European aggression against my ancestors, has contributed to our current placement on a global level. The point is a consequence of European expansion, imperialism and colonialism, was the chattel enslavement that reduced Africans to commodities, articles of commerce to be bought, sold, abused and traded. Yet this legacy is seldom mentioned in the wider public arena and when it is mentioned it is usually met with the old 'what you bringing all of that stuff up for'? That was a long time ago and you should forget the past and look to the future'! What exactly I am supposed to look forward to with no historical memory 'of all of that stuff' missing, baffles me, especially as I can still hear the 'fuck off back home' taunt that was offered to me by a white-man driver a few months ago in South east London, a couple of miles away from where I was born.

This said remember the other 'intelligent' royal who suggested that some African-American women, who were too 'noisy' whilst dining in the same restaurant as she was, should 'return to the colonies' or something like that. That caused a bit of outrage, I suppose, but the fact is that what Europeans like her and her royal kindred did to Africans like them, during the colonial period, was never mentioned. Could this be because Africans are, for many Europeans, there to serve their white mistresses and masters and then return to the kitchen? Except perhaps when the 'master' race are being philanthropic, all smiles and grins, in some mud hut or village in Africa, with a few strategically placed emaciated children 'wid fly round dem mout', posing for the camera. Could this possibly explain why in their endeavours to deflect attention away from Harry's Nazi gaff, the sympathetic elements of the press dwell on the good public work he does? Demonstrating what a really nice guy prince Harry is as they reel out the old 'look at what he does for the starving children in Africa' sob, sob. You see the fact that for me the royal family are little more than a pompous, redundant, bunch of spongers par excellence is a moot point.

What is significant is that by dint of omission little consideration is given to those whose histories are denied the public voice that other groups possess, and possess quite forcefully. Let's not forget that many other groups suffered tragic losses at the hands of the Nazis during World War II, and before the early 1960s this atrocity, The Holocaust, was viewed as another tragic and inhuman genocide. In fact this is a lesson that I believe the global Afrikan family need to learn, because many like to pretend that the past does not matter when, as in the case of the little prince it clearly does. For you see when a people appreciate the importance of having a historical memory, they will do whatever they have to do to ensure that all are aware of why it is so important for them to 'never forget'. That is why Jewish communities can quash all of their religious, racial, and cultural differences to, and quite rightly so, call any individual or nation to account who dares to transgress against them, especially if they are in a position of public visibility. Similarly the Akan people of Ghana remind us in the spirit of the Sankofa Bird, which walks forward whilst craning its neck to look behind, take the time to glance back every now and then lest you forget something you best ought remember. Peace and Blessings

W. Henry, Nu-Beyond Email-out, January 2005

Whiteness is a form of conscious or unconscious power that exists within a collective psyche and also within the individual self. There are different shades of Whiteness, from conservative to liberal, conscious to unconscious, visible to invisible and White to Black to other. It is a way of thinking which is embodied within White people as the flagship of normality and a moral conscious. However, all of humanity strives to be accepted within this boundary and thus non-White people consume it. Therefore, Whiteness is Imperialism of the everyday. I am a White man and I live in Whiteness, but I compete with it and question it on a daily basis yet find it hard to relinquish. Maybe it is because it offers me too much of my identity that I cannot let go. **Dr. John Curran**

Whiteness = Glorification of European practices, customs and beliefs. **Sister Afryea**

Ah-Free-Ka: combating whiteness in the black imagination

Introduction

> White at last! Gone was the smooth brown complexion. Gone were the slightly full lips and Ethiopian nose. Gone was the nappy hair that he had straightened meticulously ever since the *kink-no-more* had first wrenched Aframericans from the tyranny and torture of the comb. There would be no more expenditures for skin whiteners; no more discrimination; no more obstacles in his path. He was free! The world was his oyster and he had the open sesame of a pork-colored skin. (Schyler, 1998:17)

> ...Now the Afrikan race, nuff problem wi face, like wi love push wi self back innah second place, black ah fight black skin what's happening, ah seh them prefer the browning to the blackening, that foolish attitude I've never understood, it's like when people them ah tell mi seh mi hair nuh good, but if you check history that notion of beauty, is ah mentality the legacy of slavery, so if you want yuh mind free, nuh worship white imagery, just put yuh race first like Marcus Garvey. (Lezlee Lyrix, Time To Make A Change, 1996)

In the cosmology of the Kamites (Ancient Egyptians) the Ka was the 'life force' that distinguished the dead from the living person, sometimes depicted as a 'second image' that complements the living entity.

Crucially the Ka had to be nourished, fed and watered, as the moment of death occurred when the Ka left the physical body. I will argue that the feeding of the Ka transcends the notion of food and drink as merely sustenance for the physical body, but also includes food for thought, based on self-knowledge, for the human mind. For this is what makes the 'living' person conscious, as in awake and aware of their social, cultural, spiritual and political environment and in control of their thought processes. Thus the feeding of the mind must be based on a knowledge of self that reflects the experiences and aspirations of a valued member of the human family. I must point out from the outset that I will not be presenting an insight into the philosophical nuances of Ancient Kemet, I will leave that to others who are far more qualified and informed than I. Rather my suggestion is that for many Afrikans our Ka is somewhat under fed, mentally and psychologically malnourished, causing much of the self-effacement that we bear witness to today. It is being fed a poisonous diet of 'all things white and beautiful' (Henry, 1996, 2005) that appears to be healthy/normal/natural, yet is ultimately that which fosters self-rejection, as the poison distorts the 'second image' rendering it a grotesquery in the Afrikan imagination. In fact:

> At the heart of this kind of thinking is the realisation by the blacks that the most potent weapon in the hands of the oppressor is the mind of the oppressed. Once the latter has

> been so effectively manipulated and controlled by the oppressor as to make the oppressed believe that he is a liability to the white man, then there will be nothing the oppressed can do that will really scare the powerful masters. (Biko, 1978:68)

Biko suggests that any meaningful engagement with this reality must rethink the strategies we use to combat this ongoing, historically rooted, nightmare scenario. It must be focused, relentless and totally uncompromising, based on a practical blak consciousness that empowers and uplifts the Afrikan, whilst 'scaring the powerful masters', thereby freeing the Afrikan personality in this place and at this time from all forms of psychological terrorism including, but not restricted to, the metaphorical 'tyranny and torture of the comb'.

De-clawing the cat!

> What is often forgotten in any discussion of the Negro's "place" in American society is the fact that it was only as a slave that he really had one'. (Jones, 1995:54)

> It is naïve in the extreme to think that you can wish away your racial identity, and substitute for it some changeable class identity or an adopted religious, identity. Furthermore, a rat doesn't cease being preyed upon just because it dresses up like a cat, and thinks it is a cat. What is done to rats will be done to it, until rats get together and cut off the claws of the cat. (Chinweizu, 1987:171)

According to Chinwezu the task of the Afrikan in this place, and at this time, is to recognise exactly what forces are being used to down-press us and then use this knowledge against them. This means there needs to be a reckoning with many of the assumptions that we generally make about self and other in a racist society. I am arguing that much of the confusion in the Afrikan imagination is based on pre-programmed thoughts that often determine 'thoughtless' action. At this point let me be clear that when I am speaking of imagination I am not speaking of unreality, or aspects of thought that can be relegated to the wishful, fanciful realm of phantasmagoria. I am speaking of a form of socialisation that is an aspect of a strategic ploy, whereby the Afrikan's consciousness is colonised as a consequence of living in Fanon's 'white world'.

Crucially for us, Chinwezu points out the terrain on which these battles for the mind will be fought when stating that endeavours to 'wish away your racial identity', for I suppose a more acceptable one are fruitless. Unless of course you are one of that 'elite' group who can claim 'ethnic ambiguity', which is all the craze in the USA where it is suggested in the mainstream media that many celebrities, black-faced ones as well, are beyond race. These are the celebrities whose outer appearance enables them to 'pass' for some type of non-raced individual. Generally they promote the nebulous 'Mediterranean look' that allows one to confuse Beyonce with J Lo, with Christina et al. However, what about those of us 'blacks' who are blessed with darker skin, fuller lips, gluteus maximus (big batty) and choose to sport un-barbecued hair, can we claim to be 'ethnically ambiguous'? I think not would be the obvious answer but then how does one explain the fact that many blacks do their best to distance themselves from those they most resemble the closest?

Now let me be clear that a cursory glance at documented human history will show that members of the human family have always changed their outer appearance, dyed their hair, and adorned themselves for various cultural, social, spiritual and political reasons. But what I am thinking of here is why it seems to be a problem for many people of Afrikan ancestry to accept that beauty is not the sole property of white people? Why is it that when I travel to Afrika or the Caribbean I see my brothers and sisters ravaged by skin bleaching creams and other self-effacing products? By the way, please don't mention white folk who tan themselves to a golden, cancerous hue, as it's not the same game. There are many reasons why they tan in this irrational way and some have told me they do it to look 'healthier' or to look wealthier (signifies travel to hotter climes), but I have never heard a white person suggest it is because they want to be more 'acceptable' to black folk.

Similarly I have never seen a white owned hairdressing salon's advertise that they cater for 'Afro' hair, yet you would need a calculator to count how many black owned hairdressing salons have 'Afro and European Hair' emblazoned across their shop window, and often it is incorporated in the salon's name. In fact not too far from where I live there is one such salon that specialises in 'roots' hairstyles like dread locks, which has two giant images of blonde haired white women in the shop-front window. Ask yourself why this is so and then consider for a moment:

> How can the effects of the Caucasian standard of beauty be identified in the thinking and actions of Negroes? Why observe the great vogue of hair-straighteners, wigs and skin bleaches that sprang into being! Great geniuses were at work…"After one preparation Madam, you too can have silky-straight flowing tresses just as beautiful and lovely as your pale sister. Or perhaps you require a hank of this flattering Store Bought Hair? Just come as you are and when we are finished with you—well just come in to see us—then you will be the judge!" (Cleaver, 1962:127-132)

You see the concern is not just with the external manifestations of a racially damaged brain, it is the wish to physically distance yourself from yourself without realising that you are indeed the product of 'great genius'. Take for instance one blue-black Jamaican born elder told me that whilst he accepted the term Afro-Caribbean, his ancestry was from the so-called 'Aborigines' of Australia, "there is no way I am African" he often states in public. Now I am not saying this is impossible, just highly unlikely since I know his history and lineage quite well and I am totally familiar with the area in Jamaica he hails from. A good way to appreciate the seriousness of my concerns here about how Afrikans internalise and perpetuate the 'terror' of whiteness, that haunts the black imagination, is taken from my former life as a university lecturer. It was the start of a new term and at the first staff meeting I noticed that there were three new black lecturers, one of whom did not acknowledge my presence for one calendar year. During this time I shared an office with a white colleague who whilst engaged in idle conversation informed me as to how nice and personable this individual was. I then informed him "I wouldn't know as they never speak to me and almost scraped off their face against a wall, trying to avoid my gaze in the corridor on one occasion." Taken aback by this tit-bit he enquired as to why I thought this form of selective avoidance occurred? I said "it's a consequence of whiteness and the answer is quite simple really, they suffer from what I call the Dracula syndrome. He was even more confused until I explained that Dracula avoids mirrors, as he casts no reflection, which is a constant reminder of his status as one of the un-dead. Maybe I, as the mirror, am avoided for the same reason.

Perhaps if they dared to look in the mirror they would be confronted with their status as one of the un-dead, because 'white people construct the world and are the makers and doers, the creators of culture and societies, and 'we're just here' (Scafe, 1989:17). Very simply put many of us, irrespective of racial back-ground, because of our socialisation in a hostile environment cannot stop "thinking white" (Griffin 1977, Ware 2002). Moreover, our story as black/Afrikan and what we have contributed to the world in the arts, sciences and all other areas of human endeavour for millennia, is 'hidden' in the hallowed halls of academia. Thus the unspoken suggestion that mesmerises far too many damaged souls is that to be truly valued is to be European. I explained to my colleague that this is an aspect of living in Babylon that no amount of 'white studies', by white or white-minded academics will change, unless they come to realise that:

> ...whiteness in the black imagination is often a representation of terror. One must face written histories that erase and deny, that reinvent the past to make the present vision of racial harmony and pluralism more plausible..."So institutionalised is the ignorance of our history, our culture, our everyday existence that, often, we do not even know ourselves." (hooks, 1992:172)

Fundamentally, the way whiteness works is that it dis-empowers those classified as non-white who believe, invest and are trained in the acceptance of the racial superiority of Europeans. Even more worrying is the 'institutionalised ignorance' that ensures that many Afrikans know nothing of themselves, much less the achievements of their ancestors pre chattel enslavement. That is why no matter how 'educated', some never grasp the simple truth that people are people, good, bad and indifferent and we therefore need to begin to have the right conversations. What needs to be made plain is the thought and action that fuels the idea of racial superiority that many simply accept as given. For it dominates our self-perception and has done so for at least the past three centuries, from the moment when white supremacists decided to re-make and re-classify the peoples of world to enforce their 'new world' order.

There are no superior or inferior races, which on the surface sounds pretty obvious but for the fact that the way how the world is dominated by representatives of an 8% white minority, lends credence to their supposed inherent, racial, superiority. Add to this the fact that this minority ended up colonising/controlling 90% of the planet/people/resources through terrorism, barbaric acts of genocide and the wilful destruction of any perceived threat to their mission for global domination. A consequence of which was the forced exposure to a Eurocentric/ethnocentric worldview by those who came under the yoke of racial oppression. It should then be of no great surprise that when measured by an oppressor's yardstick, racial and cultural 'others' will always come up short. More so for we who are locked into a version of history that spans perhaps four centuries of chattel enslavement, which is used to reinforce the idea of the inherent inferiority of the Afrikan. Many seldom consider whiteness as an ideal that influences their thoughts and feelings about self, because its taken-for-granted nature renders it the norm and that makes it so dangerous to all of us.

For instance it amazes me when I speak to black people who openly confess that they will never date a black person and actively seek a white partner to settle down and have children with. Without giving much thought, it seems, to the fact that whatever child they produce, in this country and time, will not be classified as white. You can get as PC as you wish, and name their offspring what you will, but the simple truth is they will get the same racialised treatment as their black parent. That is why whiteness, as an anti-human presence in the racialised imagination, needs to be considered in any discussion of outer displays of what Hutton dubs:

> Acquired Anti-Own Race Syndrome (AAQRS) [which] is the philosophy and psychology of assumed European World cultural 'superiority' expressed by African peoples in their relations with each other, and in perceiving and operating in the world. (Hutton, 1997:20)

Hutton's point is important as it allows us to think away from the damaged Afrikan individual who openly displays self-hatred and deal with the knowledge base that fuels this type of soul destroying, self-harm. Once we recognise that such behaviour has a racist-biological, philosophical and psychological underpinning, that is global in its reach and consequences, we can then begin to work out how to fight it. The point is that in our endeavours to address the issues that face us as a consequence of being Afrikans in Europe's 'new world', we often waste much valuable time, resources and energy, focusing on the symptoms, the manner in which the 'rat' is attired. Instead we must now focus on how to use the knowledge we have to, as Chinwezu suggests, 'get together and cut off the claws of the cat'.

'Whiteness as rightness'

In order to liberate the Afrikan mind we must challenge a revisionist version of history that claims that what happened to Afrikans during the genocide of the MAAFA, has no bearing on our global condition as Afrikans in the Motherland and throughout the Diaspora. For instance where my people come from in Clarendon, Jamaica, is amongst the most inhospitable terrain you can find anywhere on the Island. Until this very day there are areas that you cannot drive to and it is a fact of history that my parents inherited this existence as a consequence of chattel enslavement and its aftermath. I think any reasonable person will agree that it's not right that the enslaved were 'freed' and got nothing, yet 'massa' was compensated by the British Government for his loss of 'property', and kept 'his' land.

WHITENESS MADE SIMPLE

For all of you who come off with pitiful anti-human excuses, making out like the past does not impact the present and often determine the future, consider this. My family and I were recently on holiday in a Caribbean island and decided to visit a waterfall and 'exotic' garden that was spread over 200 acres of land owned by the direct descendants of French plantation owners. Their ancestors were given the land during the 18th century by whoever was the ruler of France at that time for loyal service to the crown. Now that for me means they no doubt brutalised my ancestors thereby making a sizeable sum for themselves and their mother country. Out of curiosity I asked a local estate agent how much a quarter of an acre of land sells for in that area and was told between twenty and twenty five thousand English pounds. Now it doesn't take a genius to work out that the descendants of these former slave masters are sitting on four to five million pounds worth of real estate. That is why for all of those black folk who embark on those made for tell-lie-vision quests to find the 'the last slave', here's a word of advice. After the descendents of your 'former' chattel slave masters have finished bleating on about 'what can I do it's not my fault that I live in luxury and you lot are suffering like the ex-slaves that you are'? Simply suggest to them that they can begin reparations by returning the bulk of the land to the descendents of those whose suffering made your present lifestyle what it is.

Ah-Free-Ka: combating whiteness in the black imagination

My parents and their generation, just like my ancestors who were chattels on the plantation, were strategically and structurally placed in a position of absolute disadvantage. Consequently what is happening in the Caribbean, Afrika and many former colonies is the people often internalise their suffering. Consequently they end up blaming themselves for their unseemly predicament, which is why you often hear Jamaicans explain their contemporary suffering away in two words: 'mi salt'. By suggesting that 'mi salt' they seem to accept that they are beset with a form of perpetual bad luck. This only works if they divorce the history of how they ended up in places like Jamaica, from their contemporary social predicament. A failure to do so will impact on their self perception and they will never understand that we, black people, are not 'salt'. Rather we were and continue to be assaulted by an enemy presence and must stop looking solely within, for answers, and focus on the external factors that militate against Afrikans worldwide. We have to be courageous enough to confront the terror of the Eurocentric worldview to begin the healing process, which is what I do in my works, hence:

> Don't feel that I'm given to exaggeration just look at the world an watch what ah galang, anywhere them go I say the European, has introduced the people to destruction, their greatest tool is mis-education, whether through the school or state religion, you don't know yourself and preach integration, then sit down and wait pon you state pension, satisfied with

> your lot, you say England's okay, if ah soh why the white man don't want to stay, the life oonuh live every striking day, is according to the game them want you to play, addicted to the TV you brain cells decay, while the white man ah plan fi lef the UK, some seh mi paranoid I seh move an go way, I have mi own worldview and I know what to say. (Lezlee Lyrix, Invest in your own land, 1992)

I remember on one occasion when I performed the above lyric a white guy came over to me and suggested I was being harsh and unfair to white folk. What he really found problematic was my suggestion that 'anywhere them go I say the European, has introduced the people to destruction'. I then challenged him to prove me wrong, and guess what he sat there thinking about it for a good while and he couldn't. I know he couldn't because behind almost every contemporary manifestation of evil that ravages this planet you will find the not so invisible, historical hand of white people/Europeans. Obviously I stand to be corrected but refuse to hold my breath whilst doing so. Like him you may think this is harsh but once you interrogate the version of reality/history that dominates the public arena and start reassessing everything you know, or even think you know openly and honestly, you will see that I am right. For instance, take any everyday concern from dwindling resources, to climate change, to starving people on the most resourceful continent on this planet, scratch away the surface and see what you are left with. However white supremacists in positions of power are clever, tricky, and devious, and through their instruments of control they distract us, highlighting the symptoms then blaming the victims for having them.

Watch the news on TV and see how often the presenters /reporters portray 'starving Africans', 'tribal Africans' or whatever 'Africans', without informing you which country in Afrika they are talking about. Moreover they hardly discuss the historical circumstances behind the present day condition of these starving/struggling to be 'civilised' nations. So Robert Mugabe is a 'tyrant' and Ian Smith was what? This is how the mainstream media outlets, control the masses with the misinformation they disseminate as 'truth', especially in the newspapers and tell-lie-vision news programmes. For example, notice when they are reporting on former colonies that are ravaged by the contemporary legacies of chattel enslavement, imperialism, colonialism or other forms of white 'paternalism', they invariably harp on about a time when the country was prosperous. But we need to consider who was prospering during these golden ages? I know for a fact that it was not the subjects of domination because they were all too often accruing the wealth that maintained this uneven set of relations. For this reason I wish to feature a sizeable extract from an online article entitled 'Kaunda on Mugabe' (2007):

> Leaders in the West say Robert Mugabe is a demon, that he has destroyed Zimbabwe and he must be gotten rid of but

this demonising is made by people who may not understand what Robert Gabriel Mugabe and his fellow freedom fighters went through, says former Zambian President Kenneth Kaunda.

In 1960, Harold Macmillan, then British prime minister, made a statement in Cape Town referring to what was taking place in southern Africa as "the wind of change."

He had correctly read the feelings of the black masses...But white people in Rhodesia rejected that wind of change and, in November 1965, Ian Smith, by force, took over in a "Unilateral Declaration of Independence". It was treason against the colonial ruler, the British monarchy. Soon Smith had arrested a number of African leaders, including Robert Mugabe and Joshua Nkomo...

We must remember the occupation by Cecil Rhodes. Rhodes removed African people from fertile lands to hilly and unfertile lands in favour of settlers. And remember that, later, while neighbours became independent, Southern Rhodesia was grabbed by white settlers, led by Smith. In the struggle, many people were killed...

Of course, there are some things which President Mugabe and his colleagues have done which I totally disagree with - for example, the police beating of Morgan Tsvangirai...On the other hand, given their experience, I can understand the fury that goes through President Mugabe and his colleagues. (Kaunda on Mugabe 2007 bbc.co.uk/Africa)

Ah-Free-Ka: combating whiteness in the black imagination

I watch a lot of news, too much in fact, but I am at pains to recall when this side of the story has been featured as a contrast to the persistent demonising of Robert Mugabe by the mainstream media. Now don't get me wrong as I know my brothers and sisters are suffering almost anywhere we are found on this planet, much of which can be rooted back to European driven chattel enslavement, imperialism and colonialism. I also know that many Afrikan 'leaders' need to be held to account for perpetrating and perpetuating our condition through human greed and corruption. My problem is with the most corrupt media on this planet telling me what to believe without revealing their ulterior, political and ideological motives. As there is one thing I have learned in this life, more so with the access we have to so much information on the inter-threat— you best believe that whilst the internet is a fantastic source of information its misuse, particularly by governments, represents the greatest threat— white supremacists are the most efficient deceivers on this planet. Simply because they have access to the global systems of domination that are readily available, to them, to make the unreal and preposterous seem real and plausible. Unsurprisingly then:

> The West still negates our sovereignties by way of control of our resources, in the process making us mere chattels in our own lands, mere minders of its trans-national interests... That control largely persists, although it stands firmly challenged in Zimbabwe, thereby triggering the current stand-off between

> us and Britain, supported by her cousin states, most notably the United State and Australia. Mr. Bush, Mr. Blair and now Mr. Brown's sense of human rights precludes our people's rights to their God-given resources, which in their view must be controlled by their kith and kin. I am termed dictator because I have rejected this supremacist view and frustrated the neo-colonialists. (Mugabe, R. 2007 '62nd Session of the General Assembly of UN, http://www.un.org/ web cast/)

President Mugabe makes known that it is erroneous to accept the words of the 'neo-colonialists' who continue to treat Afrikans as 'mere chattels in their own lands'. And if you listen to the speech which this extract is lifted from you will see that when it comes to matters of history these 'supremacists', who happen to be white develop some serious amnesia. To further endorse this salient point I remember watching a mainstream TV news item on the 60th anniversary of the British partition of India and Pakistan. It was noticeable that the reporters/presenters with inhuman regularity mention only in passing the million or more souls who lost their lives during this tragic time. Even more telling is that we are in London, the epicentre of the 'former' British Empire where all manner of historical records are kept on their 'former' colonial subjects. Yet I do not recall these news items acknowledging the Raj and the death and destruction that were meted out during the period of British rule. What this means is the non-white victims are made visible in the most literal sense, generally portrayed as the perpetrators of heinous acts of 'ethnic cleansing' against their own kind. Whilst those who were directly responsible for these acts of global genocide remain invisible, as control of the media means control of the partial truths that serve to dis-inform, thereby absolving themselves from historical accountability with statements such as:

> In a message to Pakistan Prime Minister Shaukat Aziz, Prime Minister Brown conveyed the "best wishes" of the British people and praised the strong relationship between the two countries. He said: "Today marks the 60th anniversary of Pakistan becoming a nation in its own right. I congratulate this great country and send my best wishes from the British people. I celebrate the strength of the UK-Pakistan relationship. Our history, values and hopes are, and will remain, permanently intertwined." (Brown, 2007http://news.bbc.co.uk1)

What 'history, values and hopes' is Brown talking about when deliberately failing to mention the historical suffering of those whose exploitation and murder was a by product of brutish, British rule? In other words repressed voices are muted, their stories remain hidden and what we are exposed to are the distorted, racist accounts of their former 'massas'. Take for instance these 'wise' words from Brown when he was Chancellor:

> We should celebrate much of our past rather than apologise for it. And we should talk, and rightly so, about British values

> that are enduring, because they stand for some of the greatest ideas in history: tolerance, liberty, civic duty, that grew in Britain and influenced the rest of the world. Our strong traditions of fair play, of openness, of internationalism, these are great British values. (Brogan, 2005 'It's time to celebrate the Empire, says Brown' 2005 http://www.dailymail.co.uk /articles)

Brown is fully aware of the ramifications involved in formally apologising for Britain's colonial past, which is why he can make such statements knowing full well that they have never done so. We therefore have to be mindful of such an approach to history as it echoes the dominant view that must be challenged regardless of the 'credibility' of the source, for:

> It would be interesting to hear how [Andrew] Roberts - or Gordon Brown for that matter - squares such grotesque claims with the latest research on the large-scale, systematic atrocities carried out by British forces during the Mau Mau rebellion in colonial Kenya during the 1950s: the 320,000 Kikuyu held in concentration camps, the 1,090 hangings, the terrorisation of villages, electric shocks, beatings and mass rape documented in Caroline Elkins' new book, Britain's Gulag - and a death toll now thought to be over 100,000.
>
> This was a time when British soldiers were paid five shillings for each African they killed, when they nailed the limbs of Kikuyu guerrillas to crossroads posts and had themselves photographed with the heads of Malayan "terrorists" in a war

> that cost 10,000 lives. Or more recently still, as veterans described in the BBC Empire Warriors series, British soldiers thrashed and tortured their way through Aden's Crater City - the details of which one explained he couldn't go into because of the risk of war crimes prosecutions. And all in the name of civilisation: the sense of continuity with today's Iraq could not be clearer. (Milne, 2005, 'Barbarity is the inevitable consequence of foreign rule' http://www.guardian.co.uk)

Are we to believe that many in positions of power and authority, with access to all forms of information, remain unaware of these unsavoury aspects of the British Empire's 'strong traditions of fair play'? When will the rulers of this 'white world' acknowledge the wrongs they have done, and continue to do, in the name of 'civilisation'? This is the reality check that non-whites in general and Afrikans in particular need, because the history of European expansion is far from 'glorious'; except perhaps for those who are willing to bask in the sordid tales of their own barbarism.

Mapping whiteness

In light of the above the simple truth of this matter is what many white people who comment on whiteness don't get, as it is not just the fact that white = power and privilege, it is the fact that many white people in positions of real power have the information to counter these distortions and fail to do so. Why this is significant is because I know that many Afrikans, I am troubled to say, will only accept 'truth' as something that comes from the mouths of Europeans. That is an aspect of our collective socialisation and the flip side is that Afrikans cannot generally be trusted, even by their own folk, simply because they do not possess the 'open sesame of a pork-colored skin'.

Many whites in positions of power are aware of this fact, use it to their advantage and then act like anyone who challenges their perspective is misinformed, paranoid or deluded. Consequently, white people are in the minds of many deemed to be the most valued and trustworthy members of the human family, despite the overwhelming evidence to the contrary. They can get away with exploiting this actuality for one very simple reason and that is the general populace, white and non-white, have been conditioned to think in this way. That is why one of the most galling things for me when I was teaching in a university setting was the knowledge that many academics know there are different sources of information, yet fail to incorporate them in their works. By doing so they would curtail some of the psychological terror that many of us encounter on a daily basis just for being in the 'wrong' coloured skin. Jensen (2005), cites one such case where a student came to his office and informed him that one of his colleagues, a white female professor, witnessed her being racially abused in her class and did nothing, weakly suggesting that a:

> A teachable moment was lost. The whole class lost out, and the Chicana student was forced to bear the burden of the white student's racial hostility. The professor failed. Why would a professor who has a commitment to social justice pass up a chance to educate and let a non-white student struggle alone like that? Again I can't know for sure, but here's my guess: The professor was afraid. Afraid not just of the tenseness and volatility of the situation, but also afraid of stepping into the fray and possibly making a mistake. (Jensen, 2005:56)

For many of us this is no big revelation, nor is the fact that in his footnotes he states that 'looking back…I failed too' explaining how for whatever reasons 'I failed in my responsibility to engage with my colleague' (2005:56). Similarly his idea that she was 'afraid of possibly making a mistake' is laughable because what has she to fear other than perhaps having to think in a way that she, like him, were not programmed to do so? Their whiteness gives them the power, whilst supplying the readymade excuses, for them to simply do nothing.

I may sound dismissive but as a mature university student I had experiences in seminars where it was difficult for me to determine whose levels of ignorance/avoidance, on the matter of racism, were the greater; those of some of my fellow students or those of some of our tutors. In such instances it is the confronting of racism as a lived experience and being forced to listen to those whose problems are generally regarded as a 'chip on the shoulder', 'pull yourself up by your boot straps', sociological abstraction, whites find hard to digest. To them I say you have stepped into the Grey zone, that space where many non-whites actively learn to navigate a hostile environment, using Du Bois 'double consciousness' as an entry and exit pass. Moreover the discomfort of uncertainty you feel during such moments will pass, once you step back into the certainty of 'knowing' you really are doing your 'best' to counter white privilege.

Another aspect of Jensen's scenario that interests me is his assumption that his colleague has 'a commitment to social justice', for this explains how such an 'ideal' maintains white paternalism. It also explains why in the most 'progressive' teaching environments this aspect of disempowerment is overlooked by educators who assume they are antiracist when in actuality they are not. If this is not the case then what is the assumption that his colleague even cares about 'social justice', much less has a 'commitment' to it based on? We all know that people can and often do say one thing and mean another, but what makes this so dangerous is the taken for granted nature of whiteness as the gift of being in the right no matter the consequences. To counter it we have to stop acting like we don't know that the only colour associated with racial power on this planet is the colour white, therefore the people who are associated in the imagination with this colour, and have the might to enforce their collective will; inevitably rule. They will continue to rule and benefit from unearned privileges unless their status as the custodians of the world is successfully challenged, with the information that is at hand to do so. Otherwise Afrikans will continue to uncritically look to Europeans for guidance and edification not knowing that all they are doing is delivering their hearts, souls, minds and resources to their greatest exploiters and oppressors.

For instance, I was not surprised that the most visible representatives, who spoke on behalf of the continent of Africa at the G8 summit, June 2007, were none other than those two bedraggled, pop stars whose names I cannot be bothered to mention. Are you telling me to seriously believe that there are no Afrikans who are qualified to articulate the concerns of the continent at 'massas' table? I think it is insulting that in this time Afrikans are considered to be the white man's burden to such an extent that anyone can speak on our behalf and the only qualification they need is white skin. Just think about the likelihood of Snoop Doggy Dog and P Diddy representing the interests of Europeans at a music festival, much less a conference that will determine the economic futures of Afrikan nations. We are constantly being duped and played like the proverbial piano and encouraged to believe an idea of reality that cannot stand up to any form of scrutiny or rigorous enquiry.

It is therefore the thought process that underpins this colonial mindset that needs to be mapped and appreciated, because Afrikans become one interchangeable group, which is why people often get confused as to whether Afrika is a country or a continent. One way to appreciate my reasoning here is based on a tactic I used on my undergraduate students when we were considering the rise of the nations who are now known as 'western' super powers. I would simply ask the students to locate them geographically on a map, and then explain to me why they are collapsed under the umbrella of the 'west'. It soon dawned on them that the 'west' is a hegemonic construct that is used to unite 'westerners' and control 'non' westerners. But this is too easy a point to make and it has been discussed in much social theory, which is why I would then point out to them that according to the geological criteria used to determine a continent, the continent we know as Europe does not exist. I defy anyone to tell me where Europe really begins and Asia ends (I know about the Ural mountains in Russia theory as the 'dividing' line), or why soccer teams from Israel can play in the European cup, when Israel is clearly not in Europe? Europe is a part of Asia, hence the name Eurasia and the logic behind white people being formerly known as Indo-Europeans, which from the time they concocted their system of racial division has been replaced by Caucus-Asians.

Reasoning with my students in this way enabled me to explain to them that whiteness is an organising principle that was used by white supremacists to plan a world and future without, in my opinion, many non-white people in it. The proof is in the proverbial pudding when you realise how many civilisations and cultures Europeans have wiped off the face of the earth in the blink of an eye, for that is what the past five hundred years represents in the context of human history. That is why if Afrikans were to exist our designated place was at the periphery of their imagined, geographical, future-world, which is exactly where we have ended up physically, spiritually, politically, culturally and psychologically. A good way to visualise this point is to take a cursory glance at an old map of the 'known' world because:

> By the middle of the century the new geographical view of the world had come to be taken for granted. It was given its canonical expression in the work of Mercator… Mercator's new 'projection', first used in a map in 1568…drove home the idea that the land surface of the globe was naturally grouped about a European centre. So Europe came to stand in some men's minds at the centre of the world. No doubt this led Europeans for centuries to absorb unconsciously from their atlases the idea that this was the natural order of things. Most people like to think of themselves at the centre of things…Mercator helped his own civilisation to take what is now called a 'Eurocentric' view of the world. (Roberts, cited in Hall and Bram, 1992:325)

Roberts makes known that it is normal for people to place themselves at the 'centre' of all things, which is why when you are shown a group photograph with you in it, your visage will be the first thing you look for. There is nothing wrong with doing so but we need to be cognisant of what occurs when the 'normal' is masked by a wilful disorder that has reconfigured the known world and re-presented it in the image of a dominant minority. You see, when Afrikans blindly accept the 'Eurocentric' view of the world they will embrace an idea of history where they play no active role in anything of note. Our ideas of ourselves have little to do with our historical reality, which explains how decentred one becomes when taking African inferiority as part of 'the natural order of things'. I am not suggesting that we unrealistically or quaintly try to live life as we did in all of its manifestations, pre chattel enslavement. Rather I want us to re-evaluate all that we know, or think that we 'know', about each other as inhabitants, combatants, victims, friends and enemies in Europe's 'new world'. This will enable us to purge our psyches of the inherent 'superiority' of Europeans by recognising what Fuller (1984) describes as:

> The nine major areas of people activity in the known universe: Economics, Education, Entertainment, Labor, Law, Politics, Religion, Sex and War...What happens in one area of activity affects all other areas of areas of activity. What a person does the area of "Economics" affects what that person does in the area of "Religion"-or "Sex", or "War", etc. The Racists (White Supremacists), by dominating their victims

> [Non-White people) in one area of major activity, also, at the same time, dominate them in all areas of major activity. (Fuller, 1984:21/22)

When we think about white supremacy in this way, as an ideological system based on dominating thought, which largely determines action, we are better able to make the links between our predicament and the historical processes that can be used to explain it. For once any problem is broken down into its component parts it can be solved quite easily, especially when it is a problem not of your own making. Consequently, as an Afrikan living in a European dominated society where you have little say in the 'major areas of human activity', why be surprised that you are still regarded as one of the interchangeable black racial others to the white racial self. This relationship has not qualitatively changed since the days of the chattel enslavement when as commodities we were absolutely interchangeable. If the cracker (the interchangeable white master who cracked the whip) worked/ beat/tortured/raped/brutalised their nigger/negress (the interchange-able, dehumanised, enslaved African) to death 'it' was replaced with another 'it' in much the same way as we would nowadays replace a car tyre.

What I state here may upset many but only because our imaginations are dominated by versions of our struggles that are there for our pacification. Worse still is that many of the pacifiers look like me, perhaps know the history of our struggles as well as I do, and yet consciously choose to pander to their white supremacist massas for some form of acceptance. Therefore, I am always suspicious of 'community leaders' who it seems no one bothers to ask them, where are they leading us to? You see I have met many of them in person and whilst they are content to say the right things when surrounded by black folk, put one white person in the mix and they often sing a different song. Especially when they are (s)elected to represent the various political parties that are yet to convince me they are committed to right, known, historical wrongs. These leaders will echo their massas expressions of 'deep regret' for the chattel enslavement, exploitation and grossly inhuman treatment meted out to 'our' ancestors, but will not even consider reparations in any way, shape or form. We must therefore appreciate the fact that non-white people can envelop themselves in whiteness and consciously act as agents of their own oppression, for if as I am suggesting we are considering systems of power, then many 'black leaders' are indeed white supremacists. Indeed:

> Black leaders are reluctant to measure psychopathic traits of the White race in their dealings with Blacks when there is a threat involved. For example, everywhere one finds Whites and Blacks in close proximity to each other, Whites are in control, whether it is Chicago or Zimbabwe. And our leaders rarely question this extraordinary universal phenomenon

> which defies every known statistical law of probability. (Bobby Wright, http://rbg-street-scholar-multi-media-e-zine .blogspot. com2007/8)

If Wright's trenchant observations are incorrect, then how else can we explain the black politicians who share ancestry with the historical victims of the worst crime against humanity, yet act like the pursuit of reparative justice has no bearing on 'our' current global predicament? The truth is that the reason why they are 'black politicians' and not just politicians is a consequence of this history, and if they say they represent the black communities in Britain then we should publicly hold them accountable. The white rulers of society will in this time tolerate one or two niggers/negresses as long as they can control their thoughts and actions, and the more they are seen to oppress/pacify their 'own kind' the higher they seem to rise in the massas world. Consequently, those who have this awareness, coupled with the courage to champion our struggles for social justice, must actively seek a grassroots antidote to the poisonous diet we are constantly being fed in our endeavours to slip the psychological yoke of white domination, whilst reminding ourselves that:

> Now it says here "and every white man shall be allowed to pet himself a Negro. Yea, he shall take a black man unto himself to pet and to cherish, and this same Negro shall be perfect in his sight..." The appointer has his reasons, personal and political. He can always point to the beneficiary and say.

> "Look, Negroes, you have been taken care of. Didn't I give a member of your group a big job". (Hurston, cited in Dyson, 1997:10)

Conclusion

I have argued here that there is a historical legacy of chattel enslavement, behind the treatment we receive, that is impossible to 'wish away' or escape from. It more than any other factor affects the manner in which we relate to ourselves as Afrikans and other members of the human family in all of our actions, thoughts and deeds. This is not to suggest that we use this knowledge as an excuse for our continued failures, it is just to recognise that our current predicament did not come about by accident, it is part of our 'structural placement' in a world where the power over the many rests in the hands of the few. Significantly, after hundreds of years of reinforcement by various racialised systems of domination and social control, the imagination of many blacks is haunted by this legacy, which is the bane of Afrikan communities globally.

Consequently, many utilise phenotypic differences to distance themselves from all things black/Afrikan, whilst others engage in discursive debates about what it means to be Afrikan/black, under the banner of an Africentric blackness that excludes the terror of whiteness, in their endeavours to wake the dead and manifest Ah-Free-Ka. For as Garvey stated:

Ah-Free-Ka: combating whiteness in the black imagination

> We are going to emancipate ourselves from mental slavery, because while others may free the body, none but ourselves can free the mind. Mind is your only ruler, sovereign. The man who is not able to develop and use his mind is bound to be the slave of the other man who uses his mind. (Garvey: 1937, 2003 back cover)

> Whiteness makes many whites: Arrogant, Deceitful, Judgmental, Clueless, War mongers, Vicious, Merciless, Spiritless, Filthy, Hypocritical, Envious, Wannabes, Follow fashion, Dictators, Backstabbers, Thieves, Liars, Distorters of the truth. Basically, their past dictates their future. **Brother Rob**

2007 REMEMBERING THE PAST TO SAFEGUARD THE FUTURE

> History should not be hidden under the cloak of racism and prejudice. Truth is bound to be the final victor irrespective of all the desperate attempts by the Europeans and their cohorts to distort, hide or destroy Afrikan peoples' achievements. (Osei, 2006, www.blackbritain.co.uk)

> History is a set of lies agreed upon. Napoleon Bonaparte

> I find all other peoples preparing themselves for the struggle to survive, and you, still smiling, eating, drinking, dancing and sleeping away your lives, as if yesterday were the beginning of the age of pleasure. Marcus Mosiah Garvey

Greetings.

2007 is going to be a dread year for peoples of Afrikan ancestry, irrespective of where we find ourselves, as members of the human family, on this planet. For this reason I opened with a quote from

Osei who sums up what needs to be remembered in what is a unique event in world history. The global recognition that something was done to peoples of Afrikan ancestry largely at the hands of 'Europeans and their cohorts'. As Afrikans we must seize this moment and use it as a catalyst for reparative change, if we truly seek to right historical wrongs and not get caught up in the blame game that usually places penal systems of enslavement, or debt peonage on the Afrikan continent as the main reasons for chattel enslavement, a theme that will dominate much that we will be exposed to in 2007. This explains why we must be cognizant of the fact that what Afrikans will be bombarded with, throughout 2007, will be a 'set of lies' that are rooted in historical falsification and propelled by a global mainstream media that is white dominated, Eurocentric and racist. That is why we are being fed a diet of William Wilberforce as 'our' saviour and several, Government linked or funded, 'Wilberfest' events will take place on March 25th 2007 to 'celebrate' 200 years of the abolition of the so called 'trade' in African chattel slaves.

I have heard tales of plans to float flowers on the River Thames, spending in the region of 1.25 million pounds, sterling, to place a head stone in a park in central London and several very public events where black faced, celebrity show ponies, will be accepting carefully worded, 'apologetic' themed statements with full media coverage of course. The largest being the preacher led singing, dancing and praying services that will dominate the national broadcast networks in the name of CHURCHIANITY, that will do little to address the real issues the Afrikan faces as a consequence of the MAAFA. The Afrikan Holocaust of chattel enslavement. For these and other reasons many grassroots organizations in the UK have mobilized themselves to collectively challenge the latest, institutionally sanctioned, assault on our humanity, rooted in white supremacist thought and action. One such organization is London based LIGALI, who together with the Bristol based Operation Truth and a coalition of other Africentric organisations are spearheading TRUTH 2007. Their representative Toyin Agbetu states:

> The only weapon that will successfully counter this state sanctioned act of revisionist history is education. It remains an unequivocal fact of Truth that not a single enslaved African was freed as a result of the passing of the 1807 act. All good people of moral conscience should refuse to celebrate the bicentenary of an act which whilst limiting the trafficking of enslaved Africans still supported the institution of slavery. Truth 2007 exists to prevent the miseducation deliberately caused by media propagation of both Abolitionist and Wilberfest myths.

Hence if 2007 is going to mean anything at all it must be used as a catalyst to effect real change in the way the Afrikan is presented as a member of the human family because, as LIGALI argue, the media and schools ensure we only receive a 'revisionist history'. Thus those who are aware of the differences in our history must do our best to make these crucial differences known, with whatever resources we have at our disposal. For instance, more often than not you will hear crass comments about slavery as a fact of all human experiences, which all people have gone through at some point in their history. However 'no other members of the human family were subjected to a uniquely constructed notion of difference, sanctioned by laws', (Henry 2006:36) that equated the African to 'three-fifths of a human being' (Anderson, 1997:47) and no other group has had to combat this 'mathematical equation'. Add to this the impact of the 'Dred Scott Judgement' of 1857—a full fifty years after the so called abolition of slavery—which stated that Afrikan people 'blacks' were not human but 'merely articles of commerce' and 'were so far inferior that they had no rights that a white man was bound to respect' (Mullane, 1993:132).

Those who have this historical awareness must seek to redefine the terms that perpetuate their oppressed status, both literally and psychologically, and equally refuse to accept that our battle for self can be confused with other struggles against oppression. I suggest this because 2007 cannot be reduced to a conversation about the horrors of chattel enslavement alone, because this will delude people into thinking that because we no longer witness the mass kidnapping, raping, lynching and burning of Afrikans, things have improved. In fact according to Brother Hakim: 'who said slavery was done? The slave master never said he retired. He's just changed the game'. One aspect of 'changing the game' was an example of a modern day lynching, as pointed out during a recent UK lecture tour by California based Keidi Obi Awadu, The Conscious Rasta, when he presented a HIV poster that stated . 'HIV is a black disease. GET TESTED.

Can you imagine what would happen if any other racial group were placed on public display in this pathological way? You probably can't and the reason for this is that the Afrikan is globally and collectively regarded as too weak to do anything about such displays of overtly racist, dehumanising, propaganda. That is why 2007 must be about repairing the physical, spiritual, cultural and psychological damage that has placed the Afrikan in a position of disadvantage, in this place and at this time. I would encourage people to be mindful of one-off 'celebrations' and other events that uncritically accept the dominant version of history and to support events that seek to educate, empower and uplift.

One such event: ABOLITION 200: 2007 REMEMBERING THE PAST TO SAFEGUARD THE FUTURE organised by Race Equality Action Lewisham (REAL), Lewisham Ethnic Minority Partnership (LEMP), Lewisham Council and Nu-Beyond Ltd: Learning By Choice, will take place in the London Borough of Lewisham on 25th March 2007. This event, the first of many, is not about embracing victim hood or blaming the white man for every ill in the world, some of us do a grand job of perpetuating our own oppression, unwittingly or otherwise. Rather this event will be about empowerment and healing as we recognise that many wounds will be opened due to the information and misinformation we will all be exposed to from various quarters during 2007. Thus in closing I wish to leave you with the following words that eloquently capture the ethos behind our endeavours to tell our own stories:

> My wish is that the information will permeate the national curriculum and educational institutions alike, so that all may gain a deeper insight and appreciation of the insidious nature of the transatlantic slave trade and its impact on our national, international and cultural heritage. It should therefore be our aim that the commemorations are meaningful, respectful, and used as a source of empowerment for all involved. Remembering their Past to Safeguard their future and as a result the future of their children's children. (Tracey Jarrett, LEMP Co-ordinator, 2007)

Dr. Lez Henry. Published in New Nation, March, 2007

WHITENESS MADE SIMPLE

Superstition

You may try to deny my very existence,
I laugh at your feeble attempts at resistance,
writing me off as a rage in the stone age,
saying I can't exist if people resist,
that's a joke, and you know it's true,
you'll find my mark on all of you,
alchemy, magic, harvest festivals,
Stonehenge, Druids, pagan rituals,
open your eyes and you'll soon realise,
I can be found in all walks of your lives,
when you walk under that ladder that feeling of doom,
be careful tonight cause there's a full moon,
unlucky thirteen no spilling of salt,
seven years bad luck a broken mirror's fault,
you feel safe in your religion so you openly scoff,
whilst hiding behind books to ward me off,
so bibles are opened with pages marked clearly,
protected from ghosts by the ghost you love dearly,
tape measures on doors to measure your sin,
chanting psalm 13 case satan come in,
or the Obiah worker who shout out mi DEH YAH
yuh tell dem BACK OFF I'm protected by prayer,

but the more you resist the more pleasure I take,
stalking you and watching you quake, with fear,
as you look behind, afraid I'll creep up and steal your mind,
Superstition

Lezlee Lyrix **: Thacker, BBC Film soundtrack, 1992**

Orlando Atheist - To quote myself: "For man hath written this tome called the Bible in all his foolishness. Let he who overcomes superstition reap the fruits of knowledge." (www.topix.com/forum /cit/orlando-fl)

Crouching niggers, hidden crackers: we're in a 'white' mess-iah

Introduction

> God is whatever color God needs to be in order to let people know they're not nobodies, they're somebodies. James Cone

> All the laws of Washington and all the bayonets of the Army cannot force the Negro into our homes, our schools, our churches. Strom Thurmond

> There is no point in blindly following the white messiah then wondering why you are in such ah mess-iah! (Henry, 2007, Fighting The Wilberfarce)

A few years ago, I think it was around 1985, it dawned on me that the majority of what I thought and articulated, when reasoning and reflecting on my life circumstances, was couched in Judeo Christian sensibilities. In fact it was one day when I was listening to a lyric I wrote about chattel enslavement that I realised the extent to which my mind had been colonised by 'alien' theology. To my mind the colonisation of my consciousness had two distinct strands that I could readily identify. Firstly, there was what I call direct colonisation, which took place through the regular doses of white-man religion I received that served one main purpose, indoctrination. A form of indoctrination that included, but was not limited to, attending Sunday School until my early teens, watching religious programming on TV, and an over exposure to RE (Religious Education) that was compulsory when I was at secondary school during the late 1960s to early 1970s. Secondly, through what I call indirect colonisation; by this I mean being immersed in British culture which is 'Christian' to the core so a 'natural' way to make sense of the world was through this lens. For instance, 'knowing' that a Church, any church regardless of denomination, was God's house where 'all' are welcome and believing that the 'factual' programmes I saw on TV were objective truths; never questioning the fact that many were/are couched in Christian sensibilities and designed to propagate the idea of civilised whites 'saving' uncivilised blacks.

Consequently, these taken for granted aspects of my mental colonisation/socialisation, that in essence reinforced my common-sense ideas about making 'right' choices, were made without me really questioning the basis of what makes such choices 'right'. I found this revelation particularly disturbing for various reasons. Perhaps the most troublesome one was how intolerant this Judeo Christian influence made me towards my fellow human beings. Especially any who partook in un-Christian practices, which included embracing Islam, Hinduism, Buddhism, Santeria, Vodun, Obiah, and to some extent indigenous Afrikan belief systems that are generally reduced to witchcraft. I vividly recall as a teenager trying to understand why a West Afrikan school friend did not have a 'Christian' name, and feared for his future prospects. Remember until quite recently in the UK you were required to state your 'Christian' name (which has now become your forename) when filling out forms, as this was a mark of your level of 'civilisation', which explains why so many racial/cultural 'others' still insist on 'branding' their children in this fashion.

I state this was disturbing because I was introduced to my 'self' as an Afrikan in 1972 (see chapter 5) and always thought I was cognisant of the psychological damage that was caused to Afrikans by European Christians. I thought I understood that as Afrikans we were the recipients of the worst act of 'unacknowledged', racial, cultural, spiritual and political genocide in documented, human history. I thought I was aware of how as 3/5th 'human' chattel slaves we were deliberately brainwashed into 'accepting' anything that did not look like 'us' as the fully human 'saviours' of 'us'. I know that as a teenage parent I deliberately shielded my children from white imagery as best I could and encouraged them to love themselves as Afrikans.

I also recall questioning my dear mother about the 'white Jesus' who was the 'head' of the family household. I also know that I was fortunate enough to reason with many Rastafari—those who taught me personally and through Reggae music that I was an Afrikan—about why we must embrace Garvey's notion of 'seeing God through the spectacles of Ethiopia'. This meant I understood, or thought I understood, that we must challenge the idea that the only way to become fully 'human' and to know 'God' was to identify with the religious symbolism of our greatest oppressors. Yet with all of this knowledge and awareness I still couldn't shake off this mind-shackle that was Judeo Christianity. I was essentially one of the 'crouching niggers', hiding behind scriptures, afraid to challenge the rife racism that underpinned my 'belief' in God. That was until the day when I consciously began to separate the divine from the whiteness that shrouds Christianity's Eurocentric/ethnocentric world view.

I will therefore present a frank discussion on the damage done to many Afrikans/black people who it seems in this day and age, are willing to accept any white 'saviour' on 'face' value alone. I believe it is time for Afrikans, especially those of us in the 'West', to discuss the often unquestioning acceptance of white-man religion and its role in our continued oppression and pacification, without worrying about who gets upset or whose feathers we ruffle. Thereby revealing the manipulative presence of the 'hidden crackers' whose sole purpose is the maintenance of their system of global domination; that which obscures the revolutionary potential of a belief in the divine that has played a central role in every black struggle for liberation from white oppression.

Denominations or Demon-In-Nations? Turning us fool against ourselves

Now you can use up the scissors or you use up the comb, that's your prerogative but leave the dread lox alone, over Rastafari influence the Lyrix has grown, ah them mek mi know seh Afrika it ah mi home. Mi never learn bout Afrika from no preacher, mi never learn bout Afrika from no teacher, mi learn bout Afrika from some true Rasta, like mi sister Asher, Cosmo and Shaka.

Mi head top lox but I don't wear tam, don't eat bacon Lyrix don't eat ham, look to the mother land fi draw mi inspiration, nah go ah church and call mi self Christian, too much hypocrite out deh ah lead the sermon, ah talk bout peace and love to each and everyone, but all that change when them see the Rastaman, hear them, cut off you dread an have ambition, then come innah mi church fi you salvation, but don't bother come without a donation, now all preacher man I'm asking one question, ah which youth born with ah comb innah them hand?

...Nuff people love to fight against Jah Rastafari, tru nuff ah smoke sess an hail Selassie I, The Lion Of Judah Son of The Most High, them have ah problem and seh the Rasta too lie, cause everybody know, it's just ah plain fact, that Jesus Christ him could ah never be black, because ah preacher tell them this and preacher know the most and them have them white Jesus picture in them house, well any preacher tell you this ah them you nuh fi follah, when Christ did ah walk them never

> have no camera, and the white Jesus to who nuff black head ah bow is ah family portrait from Michael Angelo, commissioned by the pope so that Rome couldah rule, them tek Christ as ah tool fi tek the people tun fool, so if you have ah saviour, that you no favour, you better tek it off the wall and go look innah the mirror. (Lezlee Lyrix, Scissors & Comb, 1989)

By now you will have noticed that on the front cover of this book is an image of myself and 'Jesus', taken in a high street on a warm autumn afternoon in Toronto Canada in the year 2000. The photo was taken by a teenaged relative who lives in Canada and was in the midst of showing me the sights when we were accosted by my 'Christ like friend'. I say accosted because as we walked past him he shouted 'fornicator' and I enquired as to whether he was talking to me. 'Bold as brass' he nodded in the affirmative. Now as I was in a bit of a hurry, we were on our way to catch a store before it closed, I simply asked 'Jesus', "are you gonna be here for a while", to which he replied "yes" so I assured him "mi soon come back". When I returned 'Jesus', and an identically attired 'Jesus' colleague who was on the opposite side of the road, were still patrolling the high street. So I gave the young lady my camera and told her to take some pictures of me and 'Jesus' and to watch his demeanour change once I start to reason with him. Incidentally I did not bother to ask him why he called me a 'fornicator' as I sussed out that as I was walking with a teenager, and did not have on a wedding band, he put two and two together and came up with one almighty mistake. Rather, what I did was to simply ask him "are you Jesus?" He did not answer but sought to engage me in a theological discussion by trying to find out whether I was Rastafari. I ignored this obvious ploy to distract me and asked him "why are you dressed like that mate are you Jesus?" Again he failed to answer what for me was a reasonable question and thus our 'dialogue' continued in this fashion for about five minutes or so. Every time he mentioned Biblical scriptures or tried to get me to discuss the contents of the flier he gave me, I would just ask him the same questions.

It was noticeable that less than a minute into our conversation 'Jesus' was becoming more and more irate at my persistent questioning, until, as we say in Jamaica, 'him swell till im buss'. At which point he started raising his voice and condemning me to all forms of hell and damnation, to which I told him to "just cool yuh self, son of man" as I didn't see the need for him to get so upset. I then said "since you won't answer my questions can I assume that you are not Jesus and if this is the case how can you believe in 'God' and then dress like a 'graven image'?" This only served to infuriate him further and I could see my niece getting worried, so I bid 'Jesus' farewell and turned and began to walk away; remaining circumspect of course because growing up in a racist society I have learned not to turn my back on an angry white man no matter how 'well-dressed' he may be.

As I did so he began shouting louder and louder, hurling even more furious, scriptural, condemnations at me. My niece was gobsmacked by what she had witnessed and when we were on our way and well out of earshot she asked me how I knew he would react that way. The answer I gave her is quite simple.

In my opinion that guy like anyone else, black or white, who tries to convince Afrikans in this day and age that 'Jesus' looked like that are white supremacists and this is why. You will notice that in the lyrical extract above, I question the role of such imagery in our everyday lives and ponder why a people who were deliberately brain-washed by white, 'Christian' racists, still freely choose to embrace an image of a 'saviour' who does not look like them. I find this especially concerning since recently a Nigerian friend of mine showed me her prayer/hymn book that is written in Yoruba with an English translation. Yet the first image you see is someone who looks like the 'Jesus' I met in Canada, with the picture of an African man on the next page. I then asked my friend what would happen if she covered the white Jesus with say a picture of a family member, or anyone who looks more like her, which is what I would do if I was in that situation? Suffice to say the subject was changed.

I find this occurrence both disturbing but completely understandable, when we recognise that a global minority control the media and thus dominate the global majority. For instance, the self-styled

'Jesus Project' actually provides communities, in the remotest regions of the planet, with the necessary equipment to watch their 'Jesus' film, which is known:

> As one of the most effective evangelism tools with more than 6 billon viewers globally over 28 years, the "Jesus" film has been seen and translated far more times than top Oscar-winning films such as "Gone With the Wind," "The Sound of Music," and "The Wizard of Oz."
>
> When the 1,000th translation milestone is reached, the one million primarily Ho speaking people in India will be able to hear the Gospel story in their "heart language." Already through the film more than 200 million people have accepted Christ as their Savior.
>
> The 'Jesus' film is life-changing for so many reasons," Jim Green, executive director of The JESUS Film Project, said in a statement. "As viewers see the compassion of Jesus and hear His Word in their own heart languages, they are drawn to Christ. As Jesus said, 'When I am lifted up, I will draw all people to Myself'. (www.christianpost.com/articleJesusFilm)

I think it is pretty obvious that this idea of being 'drawn' to their 'savior' goes hand in hand with losing the 'battle' for your 'hearts and minds' for at least two reasons. Firstly, you will have one bag of white biblical personages acting out scenes from a book that has nothing to do with your indigenous belief systems. Secondly, in my view even more perniciously, these white personages will colonise your consciousness by speaking to you in your own "heart languages." This is what I believe needs to be explained with regards to how whiteness works, because if the white Jesus image was not there and you only received the 'word', in your "heart languages", you would naturally conceptualise the divine in your own image. More importantly, you wouldn't be exposed to an 'alien' image speaking directly to you in your "heart languages" as a deliberate ploy to alter your worldview and your place at the centre of it.

The fact that they have the means at their disposal to translate the scriptures into 1000 different languages means that they focus on the film's soundtrack and not the visual aspect. Therefore, if their concern was to merely spread the 'Word of Jesus', why not just provide those who need to be 'saved' with the soundtrack in their "heart languages"? Why is it necessary for these groups to 'see the compassion of Jesus' in the image of a white man? You don't have to be a multi-genius like Imhotep, to fathom out what the deal is here where whiteness is concerned.

Moreover, the disseminators of this form of propagandist indoctrination, which leads to self-alienation, are almost certainly aware that the white God/Jesus/biblical imagery that globally dominates, can easily be traced to specific historical moments. Not wishing to belabour this point, suffice to say that the imagery featured in 'Michelangelo's Ceiling' (1509-1512), which dominates the Sistene Chapel in Rome is amongst the most famous. However, and of even more significance to this discussion is the fact that over four hundred years later it was Warner Sallman's ubiquitous 'The Head of Jesus Christ', that is responsible for making the image of a white Jesus a global, household feature. Sallman's 1940 oil painting has become the largest mass produced image in history with well over 500 million copies distributed worldwide. So here we have a reality check as to why these white images of 'our' saviour are so globally dominant and physically inhabit non-white spaces. Besides, the 'Jesus' I met in Canada is based on Sallman's image, which is not surprising as every American soldier was given a copy of this image during World War II, which partially explains how it became so globally recognisable. Yet the holy book that invariably accompanies the image unequivocally states:

> Their idols [graven images] are silver and gold, the work of men's hands. They have mouths, but they speak not: eyes have they, but they see not: They have ears, but they hear not: noses have they, but they smell not: They have hands, but they handle not: feet have they, but they walk not: neither speaks them through their throat. They that make them are like unto them; [so is] every one that trusteth in them. (Psalms 115:1-8 Holy Bible)

Crouching niggers, hidden crackers: we're in a 'white' mess-iah

I find it fascinating that when I mention such scriptures to black people who are into the white imagery, many try to convince me that it does not affect them in any way. Oh yes, and for the benefit of you 'clever' ones out there just substitute 'silver and gold' with 'canvas', 'Polaroid' and 'celluloid' and you will get the general point, which is about questioning the role of the image as too many blacks feel they need to worship it to know God. That is why so many of us grew up with these 'graven images', seldom being allowed to question their invasive 'alien' presence for fear of having the devil slapped out of us. Fact is there were no members of my family, living in our household, who even remotely looked like that so if God, literally as we are led to believe created man in his own white 'image' where did we fit in? That is why Afrikans need to consider the lunacy of worshipping such imagery and the ramifications of such 'mindless' deeds in this dread time. For, in truth, the people who are the perpetrators of the worst acts of racial genocide against people who look like me look like that image, hence:

> Don't seduce to reduce wi knowledge, cau I will always break down those barriers an bun down bondage, oh lord God almighty grant all privilege, I have to overcome all wicked, dem an dem false tings. I have no white god, don't teach me anything wrong would yuh white god save me from white man oppression, I have no white god, it's just ah black messiah, if ah white god ah bless how him nuh bless Siz. I have no white

> god, don't teach me anything wrong would yuh white god save me from white man oppression, I have no white god, it's just ah black messiah, if ah white god ah bless how him nuh bless Siz.
>
> I want what's rightfully mine soh mi nah stay mute, your system was designed to distract me from di truth, but it will come to pass an known unto di yout, in the process of time we will know di truth, you give we white god tuh praise in slavery, di doctrine carry on into black community, the black messiah yuh try to shield with fantasy, but wi nah goh mek yuh destroy di love with luxury, have to touch home I have no place in Babylon, as I go they make me victim of their unjust action, I won't be conquered in this region, I have to stand and go strong. (Sizzla, True God, 1994)

Sizzla reminds black people how we ended up in a world where we freely worship the 'white god' and join 'Christian' groups who used their 'relig-wrong', according to Rastafari teachings, to control us on the plantation. It is prudent for me to make this known because the significance of the teaching and preaching of Rastafari is a crucial factor in many of the global struggles for black liberation. That is why in the opening lyrical extract I demonstrate how central their reasonings were to my own cultural development and Sizzla endorses this point when stating any image we have of a 'black messiah yuh try to shield with fantasy'. If you cannot conceptualise God in your own image you will remain a pawn to anyone who has the power to 'distract you from the truth'. I explicitly deal with this aspect of the struggle in my lecture-presentations where I analyse a series of images, explaining the process behind how we went from Afrikan 'self-reverence' to European 'other-reverence'. I begin such discussions with an image of the Great Sphinx in Giza, Kemet/Egypt, which is over six thousand years old and bears no resemblance to any European/Caucasian—despite its regular 'face lifts'—to demonstrate one of the best visual examples of Afrikan, divinely inspired, 'self' love. I then show the DVD cover from the TV film 'Roots' and ask those in attendance if they remember the scene where, in the dark of night, Afrikans are seen holding aloft a new born baby as part of a welcoming ceremony. This obviously symbolises a link between the child's parents, their kith and kin, their ancestors and the divine order; the giver of all life. I then explain that this practice is in line with the Afrikan principle 'I am we', or 'I am because we are, because we are therefore I am', which means there is an acknowl-

edgement of a divinely inspired collective responsibility that transcends the needs and wants of the individual.

At this point I juxtapose this Afrikan philosophical principle with one taken from the highly influential French, Enlightenment, philosopher, René Descartes' "Cogito Ergo Sum - I think, therefore I am." A Eurocentric ideal that privileges the individual over the collective which was made flesh in ex Prime Minister Margaret Thatcher's famous saying, "there is no such thing as society. There are individual men and women, and there are families." I make these comparisons to increase our awareness of the psychological differences between a Eurocentric and an Africentric perspective on what it basically means to be human. I am not suggesting that this is the sole measure of these racial groups, but one thing that cannot be denied is that every European nation involved in the chattel enslavement of my ancestors used Christianity to justify their inhumanity. The point is that before the advent of Christianity, Afrikan peoples had various philosophical systems that provided them with a collective sense of belonging. Not just to each other as members of the human family, but also to the divine, which 'we' believe created all things, in and at all times. Europeans did their level best to erase these principles from the Afrikan psyche and replace them with a culture of dependence on them as veritable gods on Earth. It should therefore be noted that:

Crouching niggers, hidden crackers: we're in a 'white' mess-iah

> The Christian statement, as an established aspect of European culture, is, after all a nationalistic ideology (in that it is an expression of the ideology of a particular culture just as any religious statement is), and its function in this regard is to serve the interests of that culture. The docility and lack of aggression of the conquered peoples serves this interest, and so the Christian directive is dual in nature; while it provides the justification for a world order in the service of a European god, its teachings encourages others to be non-political and discourages their cultural nationalism (identification with their gods and belief systems). (Ani, 1994:143/4)

Ani points out that as Afrikans we cannot divorce European culture from the ideological systems that underpin its religious belief systems. To embellish this point the next item I display is this image of 'Freedom as a gift from Christ' in Suriname, formerly Dutch Guiana (Jetses in Pieterse, 1992). Notice the Afrikans are no longer holding the child up to the universe for the reasons I stated before. Rather they are now holding their baby up to an image of a white Jesus, not just to welcome their child into the human family, but also to sanction the 'gift' of 'freedom'

they received from the heavenly representative of the people who enslaved them in the first place. The point is that unless as Afrikans we have these discus-sions and really begin to interrogate much of what we believe, and who we believe in, we will continue to be suckered by those who recognise our belief in God as a means to enrich themselves. For instance, I was in the USA recently and saw a white 'Televangelist', selling what looked to me like coloured flannels that supposedly had some mysterious healing qualities, which were for sale of course (I know some of you are checking your cash flow before you seek him out online). Even more worrying was the congregation seemed to be predominantly black, rolling around, and getting completely out of themselves whenever he went anywhere near them. Now this guy may well be sincere, that is a moot point; what I want to know is when did possessing a piece of cloth, become necessary to Christian salvation?

The answer is when it was introduced to the congregation as a necessary requirement by God's representative on earth. Likewise I know black people in the UK who are as broke as hell, struggling to make ends meet, but will pay by instalments to download an overly expensive, interactive version of the bible that is being hyped by, you guessed it, another white evangelist. I will leave you to guess the race of the central figures in this version, as this is just another example of 'us' being the masters of perpetuating our own oppression. I must state that whatever a person does to access the divine is up to them, but if you are an Afrikan embracing Christianity, maybe it is prudent for you to consider Cooke's suggestion:

> Just as how I believe in reading the Bible from the beginning, I believe that we should try as best as possible to know African history from the start, from Alkebu-lan; beginning from Marcus Garvey and Martin Luther King Jnr. just does not cut it. Allied with this blanking out of Africa before "Dr. Livingstone, I presume" is a softening of what white people have done to African people. It is so sanitised. (Cooke, (2003) 'Black History sanitized', www.gleaner.com/

Cooke demonstrates why it is so dangerous for Afrikans to blindly accept that the solutions to our collective problems can be found in the Bible alone. In fact it would be sheer folly to do so since it would mean cutting off the possibility of learning about the history of Afrika when it was known as 'Alkebu-lan'; 'one of the original names for the African continent, meaning "Garden of Eden," "Mother of all Mankind," and "Garden of God."' (www.O'ia-daInternational, Inc, 2006/7). It is important to make this point because once we research and reclaim our known historical contributions to world history, especially where religion is concerned, it will be easier for us to reject the Caucasian imagery used to 'sell' their brand of white Christianity to us. That is why I argue that no representation is better than misrepresentation, for I know that if you are an Afrikan and a Caucasian tried to convince you that a picture of them was indeed a picture of you, being of sane and sound mind you would naturally reject their suggestion outright.

"Cleave to the black": freeing the mind, saving the self

If we are to free our minds from worshipping whiteness and reclaim our consciousness of who we are, what we have achieved, and what we have become, we have to be prepared to challenge anything that is to our collective detriment. Take for example an article I noticed in the Voice newspaper, entitled "HOLY, 'MARY', Maligned misunderstood" (Wilson, 2007) which featured all white biblical imagery. I find it perplexing that he could use this imagery in a piece that is questioning the authenticity of biblical doctrine, but fails to consider that these biblical personages do not necessarily reflect the target readership of a black newspaper. I know many will still say 'Jesus no have no colour', to which I say well don't depict him at all then, especially in a newspaper that is trying to raise the self-esteem of the descendants of enslaved Afrikans. If you still don't see the relevance of this then consider that all of the 'slave ships' were sanctioned by the religious rulers of the various European nations, and many carried names like 'The Good Ship Jesus' which was in fact 'The Jesus of Lubeck'. Consequently various Eurocentric institutions that propagated the idea that they were 'civilizing the savages', justified 'civilization and progress' both scientifically and religiously.

An attitude that has been a constant from the earliest period of colonial contact, exemplified in the words of one of the most famous 'privateers', Sir Francis Drake 'their gain shall be the knowledge of our faith. And ours such riches as the[ir] country hath' (Chinwezu1975:1). What we may ask, could lead Drake to believe that the various 'peoples' he encountered would gain from European knowledge and faith? The answer is partly provided by Montesquieu who suggests: 'it is impossible for us to suppose that these beings should be men; because if we supposed them to be men, one would begin to believe we ourselves were not Christians' (West, 1982:61).

Consider how these 'intellectuals' use the simplest of ideas to justify their inhumanity, but what is truly significant for us is that they use Christianity to bolster their claims of superiority, safe in the knowledge that whatever is done to these 'beings' is the will of the white god of their faith. Thus it is unrealistic for us to ignore the reality that white dominated religious, political, and cultural constructs, that are in essence anti-Afrikan, have on our psychological make-up. Worse still, many Africans are aware of the culpability of certain 'demon-in-nations', with regards to their brutal and significant role in the chattel enslavement of our ancestors, and still blindly follow them.

For instance, groups like the Mormons who openly teach that 'black skin' is a curse from their god; they can revise and amend their books as much as they like to suit a non-white audience, but a cursory glance at their leader's 'revelations' will bring the sensible hurtling back to reality. For not only did they preach that black skin was accursed, for them and many other 'demon-in-nations', it was their divine duty as white people to execute God's will by carrying out his judgement and enslaving Africans.

Imagine associating yourself with such groups, whose advocates were rejected when they first went to Africa during the early 1960s, yet today they have allegedly 200,000 black members worldwide. Many of whom are in the USA where they have had black Mormons for decades (put black Mormons in your favourite search engine and see who comes up). I find it incredible that blacks in the USA, Afrika and the Caribbean can embrace this 'alien' white-man tradition, and in the context of the UK for me it is sheer madness. You see I recall the furore caused by the 'The Osmonds'—a Jackson Five rip off white Mormon pop group from the USA, who toured the UK in the 1970s—because their beliefs forbade them from associating with black people, which led to many black youth chanting them down on Sound Systems in Reggae Dancehalls during that moment. There was no confusion for us back then as we took what came out of their mouths and used it to castigate them without apology.

Crouching niggers, hidden crackers: we're in a 'white' mess-iah

Indeed for further clarification of this aspect of my argument insert http://thecomforter.info/main/content/view/32/40/ into your preferred search engine and check out 'The Comforter and the Mormons' and note why you should not judge people on appearance alone. You see once you have consulted a wider breadth of information, on what you believe, you will naturally be in a position to make more informed choices. More informed choices means the unlikelihood of being duped by charlatans, whose power over your minds is based on them withholding vital information from you. That is why they say 'knowledge is power', without perhaps considering that knowledge gives us the power to enslave or liberate, so it's what you do with said knowledge that is important. For example, quite a few years ago I made two Mormons scamper out of a friend's house by simply asking them a few questions about their saviour's historical views on blacks and whether their 'white god' will save the 'accursed blacks' from their 'white man oppression'?

Similarly I am reminded of an altercation I had at Goldsmiths University in 1996 with a white ex South African Major General who, a couple of years after the so called end of apart-hate (apartheid), was given the position of deputy high commissioner. He emphasised the fact that he was a Christian and how great Mandela and the ANC were now that they were no longer 'terrorists'. He also spoke optimistically about looking forward to the day when 'little Mandela's' and little 'de Klerks' could play together or something like that. To be honest his speech got so 'milky' and sermonic that to save my sanity I tuned my ears out and stood there with one hand raised, awaiting the opportunity to interrogate him. When it came the first thing I did was to chastise the Student's Union for inviting him into the building, explaining that the reason why most of those in attendance were white, was because many of the black students refused to support their misguided initiative. I then let him know that I too was insulted by his presence when the situation in South Africa had not qualitatively changed for the indigenous population.

I then invited him to answer the following questions: who determines what a 'terrorist' is? How many of us have you killed under the guise of anti-terrorism? And if in fact Winnie Mandela, a real revolutionary, is a terrorist? He did not directly answer any of my questions but rather sought to justify his position by suggesting that when he was waging war against the 'terrorists' he was a soldier carrying out his duty. Adding that as a Christian he was doing what he honestly believed to be right, suggesting that I could get information on the situation concerning Winnie Mandela from the media.

I suggested that he was trying to insult my intelligence by expecting me to believe anything that comes out of a white controlled media that demonized a group of indigenous freedom fighters under the banner of terrorism?, I then pointed out that you do not erase a legacy of oppression, and all the psychological damage that goes with it, through some overnight, rhetorical acts of a new-found brotherly-sisterly love. We need to understand that what is popularly promoted as 'progressive' racial harmony, as in the case of South Africa, obscures what is happening on a grassroots level to the black oppressed. This is exemplified and embodied in this case and in the proselytizing campaigns of historically amnesic, groups like the Mormons et al. A white man is put forward as the promoter of racial harmony to suppress, silence and camouflage the voice of the black oppressed, for whom little has changed since the time when Nelson Mandela was branded a 'terrorist'. And, at his trial, stated "I do not deny that I planned sabotage. I planned it as a result of a calm and sober assessment of the political situation." I think this is what needs to be remembered in such instances as far too often, where black people are concerned, yesterday's oppressor becomes today's saviour, which is why Grant suggests:

> White supremacy only continues because we do not have the collective courage, foresight, will, unity and commitment to overthrow it. The oppressor needs the oppressed to actively work to maintain his system. Afrikans need to realise that we have become everyone's footstool and footsoldiers apart from our own, be it knocking doors for Jehovah's Witness' or killing Iraqi's for Caucasian white supremacists, we spend so

> much time doing the bidding of others we have no time to free ourselves. (Grant, 2004:62)

I agree with Grant's perspective on this aspect of the struggle and welcome his frankness, because far too much time is wasted pretending that we don't know what our collective responsibilities are. That is why many of us are content to be 'crouching niggers', awaiting instructions from the 'hidden crackers' whose greatest wish is that we remain 'everyone's footstool and foot soldiers', thereby failing to recognise the commonality of our condition. What this means is that too many of us are spending valuable energy, time, and resources, dividing ourselves along cultural and religious lines, which only serves to exacerbate the tensions between us as Afrikan peoples on the continent and throughout the Diaspora. A case in point was when I was a studio guest of Brother Geoff Schumann on his Sunday night phone-in show (May 2006) and was asked my views on some controversial comments made by a black labour politician who:

> Writing in Jamaica's Sunday Observer, Abbott said that oil-rich Nigeria had become an ecological disaster area. It was riven by religious conflict, with dozens killed in rioting over the Danish cartoons of the Prophet Muhammad which 'most Nigerians had not actually seen'. She called President Olusegun Obasanjo a 'recycled general' trying to hold office for life, and added: 'When it comes to corruption, Nigerians make

> Jamaicans, and every other nationality in the world, look like mere amateurs'.
>
> Abbott added that she had asked 'educated Nigerian Muslim women' if they favoured the sharia-law penalty of 'death by stoning' for women adulterers. 'They said yes. Whatever the educational challenges in Jamaica, you would be hard put to find women, however illiterate, who thought stoning a woman to death for adultery was correct,' she wrote... 'I see her on the Daily Politics talking about Iraq', Ogundamisi said, 'but not a word about Nigeria - in fact, not a word about Africa'. (Temko, N. 2006 "Think Jamaica is bad? Try Nigeria...How Diane Abbott enraged a community', www. politics.guardian .co.uk/labour/story)

There are a few things that concern me about the above that I think need to be addressed. For example, what model is she using to base her assessment of governmental corruption on? Surely it cannot be the British one that is so steeped in corruption and freakism that it doesn't seem to matter which so called party is in power in the United Sindom. The blatant deception, sex scandals, wanton misappropriation of funds, and subsequent resignations are commonplace, everyday occurrences. Don't even get me started on their 'legal' warmongering all over the globe that is costing the lives of countless poor souls, on all sides, in their insane pursuit for white-Christian led planetary domination. My suggestion is that if you want to understand what governmental corruption really is, then firstly analyse the behaviour of the colonial 'parents' in the 'mother country', before passing uninformed judgement on their colonised, 'bastard' children.

With this said another concern is the 'divide and rule' tactic Abbott uses in her comments, premised on an idea of 'Christian' versus 'Muslim', 'educated' versus 'uneducated', 'Nigerian' versus 'Jamaican'. We have the suggestion that even 'educated, Nigerian, Muslim, women' think 'sharia-law' an acceptable way to deal with 'adultery', but the fact is that if this is an aspect of Islam and that is the religious belief system they embrace, then why be surprised that some will hold this view?

Similarly, her views on the reaction of Nigerian Muslims over the Danish cartoons are also troubling, because unlike Christians, Muslims do not display 'graven images' as part of their faith. This means that their hostile reaction to the 'knowledge' that there is an image of the Prophet Muhammad, specifically designed to ridicule their faith, can only be explained in the context of their customs; particularly when the ridicule is coming from European 'non-believers'. I am not saying it is a right reaction. I am just saying it has to be placed in its religious and cultural context and should not be used as a way to take a cheap shot at other peoples' beliefs, for the sole purpose of dividing Nigerians from Jamaicans.

The final aspect of her commentary that I wish to deal with is the notion that Nigeria is 'riven by religious conflict' which again needs to be considered in its proper context. Take for instance the central role that organised religious belief systems like Islam and Christianity play in the lives of peoples of Afrikan ancestry, many of whom refuse to discuss the history behind how they ended up as Christians and Muslims in the first place. I wonder if they realise that:

> …the cataclysmic entrails of the export of African peoples as slaves, and the plunder of their natural resources, two crucial features that would underline the European invasion of Africa as from the 15th century, were indeed fully operationalised with devastating effects by the Arab/Muslim occupation of the continent much earlier. In this context the Arab/Muslim invasion directly paved the way for Europe's subsequent attack…For Africa, therefore, the first phase of this holocaust of a millennium was now underway, and Europe would attempt to push this process to a final solution, starting from the 15th century. (Ekwe Ekwe, 1993:5)

Ekwe Ekwe's argument is telling when we consider that the presence of many Islamised Africans was a consequence of 'Arab/Muslim invasion', before chattel enslavement. Thus the crucial religious links between these faiths became a necessary factor in the conquest, and subsequent carving up of the continent, by racist Europeans. This means that any discussion of current 'religious conflicts' has to take such factors into consideration. Otherwise we overlook the central role that firstly Arab/Muslim, and then European/Christian aggression played in the 'religious' subjugation and physical displacement of millions of Afrikans. Yet we must also be honest enough with ourselves about how we can take full responsibility for effecting solutions to our ever-present problems by recognising that 'our entrapment is often set in motion by whites but often maintained by our own people' (Asante, 1994:3). Asante suggests that we can no longer afford to 'maintain' our own 'entrapment' by simply blaming white people, or any other people for that matter, for our continued failures to liberate ourselves. What we must do is be prepared to interrogate the historical and contemporary causes of our wretched, global, condition and use the knowledge and available resources to transcend them. That is why we cannot afford to be distracted by black faced 'leaders' whose preferred occupation seems to be to exacerbate the tensions between Afrikan people, in the service of their white masters.

Conclusion

If as Afrikan members of the human family we are to make the necessary progress to liberate our minds and our continent from the shackles of 'alien' domination, one thing that we must do is separate our notions of the divine from the 'alien' presence that turns us fool against ourselves. Many may not like this suggestion but whether we like to admit it or not, a belief in the divine is central to the world-view of Afrikan people; and whilst such belief is a source of empowerment its misuse has been a major weakness. Our collective problem is that our enemies recognised this weakness, from day one, and exploited it to the full, and as stated above it continues to this very day. However this weakness can be overcome by adopting a pragmatic approach to how we have used religious belief to galvanise our efforts to resist and transcend oppression. We have done so on many occasions in the past and can do so again, because if you look historically at the revolutionary struggles for Afrikan/black liberation, they were invariably based on an idea of doing 'God's' work. A notion that can be summed up in the Baptist Deacon, Paul Bogle's rallying call, during the Morant Bay rebellion in Jamaica on October 11th 1865: we must learn to "Cleave to the black, colour for colour." Revolutionaries like Bogle, knew who the 'enemy' was based on what was being done to them as a collective and we too must recognise the root causes of our contemporary global predicament. Thus Afrikans can no longer ignore the central role that enforced religious, political and cultural constructs play in justifying our global presence as the biblical 'hewers of wood and drawers of water', as I too:

> ...have learned that my early presuppositions about White religion were not totally unfounded, because white supremacy and English religion are still bedfellows. (Beckford, 1998:44)

Index

References

Achebe, C. (1988) *Hopes And Impediments*: Selected Essays 1965 – 87 London: Heinemann International

Alkalimat, A. H. (1998) 'The Ideology of Black Social Science' in Ladner, J. (ed) *The Death Of White Sociology* Baltimore: Black Classic Press

Anderson, C. (1997) *Dirty Little Secrets About Black History, It's Heroes, And other Troublemakers*, USA: PowerNomics Corporation of America

Ani. M (1994) *Yurugu: An African-Centred Critique of European Cultural Thought and Behaviour* Trenton, New Jersey: Africa World Press, Inc

Asante, M. K. (1995) *Afrocentricity* Trenton, NJ: Africa World Press

Back. L (1987) *New Ethnicities and Urban Culture London*: UCL Press

Baldwin. J (1985) *The Price of a Ticket* New York: St Martins

Beckford. R (1998) *Jesus Is Dread Black theology and Black Culture in Britain* London: Darton, Longman and Todd, Ltd

Beckford, R. (23/9/2007)'The Great African Scandal' Channel 4. UK

Best. S & Kellner. D (1991) *Postmodern Theory* London: Macmillan

Biko, S. I (1978) *I Write What I Like* Oxford: Heinemann

References

Browder, A. (1989) *From The Browder File* Washington D.C. USA: The Institute of Karmic Guidance

Bryan. B, Dadzie. S & Scafe. S (1985) *Heart of the Race: Black Women's Lives In Britain* London: Virago Press Ltd

Bulham, H. A. (1985) *Frantz Fanon And The Psychology Of Oppression* New York: Plenum Press

Campbell, H. (1985) *Rasta and Resistance: From Marcus Garvey to Walter Rodney* London: Hansib Publishing Ltd

Carby, H. V. (1999) *Cultures in Babylon: Black Britain and African America* London: Verso

Carmichael, S. and Hamilton, C.V. (1967) *Black Power: The Politics of Liberation in America* Great Britain: Pelican Books

Chinweizu. (1987) *Decolonising The African Mind* Lagos, Nigeria: Pero Press

Coard, B. (1991) *How The West Indian Child is made Educationally Sub-Normal In The British School System* London: Karia Press

Cooper, C. (2000) 'Rhythms of Resistance: Jamaican Dancehall Culture and the Politics of Survival' Paper via email May 2000

Coard, B. (1991) *How The West Indian Child is made Educationally Sub-Normal In The British School System* London: Karia Press

Cork, L. (2005) *Supporting Black Pupils And Parents: Understanding and Improving Home-School Relations* London: Routledge

Dead Prez, (2000) 'Let's get Free' (Album), London: EMI Records.

Dent, G. (1992), (ed), *Black popular Culture* Seattle: Bay press

Dove. N, (1994) 'The Emergence of Black Supplementary Schools as Forms of Resistance to Racism in the United Kingdom' (in) Shujaa. M. J. (1994) (ed) *Too Much Schooling Too Little Education: A Paradox Of Black Life In White Societies* Trenton NJ: Africa World Press, inc.

Dyer, R. (1997) *White* London: Routledge

Ekwe Ekwe, H. (1993) *Africa 2001: The State, Human Rights and the people* Reading, England: The International Institute For Black Research.

Ekwe Ewke, H. (1994) 'The Idiocy and Tragedy of a Euroassimilationist Illusion', 'African Peoples Review' Vol III, No.2, pp16, July-September, Reading, England: The International Institute For Black Research.

Eze, E. (1997) *Race and the Enlightenment* London: Blackwell

Fanon, F. (1986) *Black Skin, White Masks* London: Pluto Press Ltd

Firmat, G. P. (1996) (in) Junot, D. *Drown* London: Faber & Faber.

References

Fuller, N. Jr. (1984) *The United Compensatory Code/System/Concept: a textbook/workbook for thought, speech and action for the victims of racism white supremacy* Fuller: USA

Gabriel, D. (2006) 'Bell Curve Theory spouted by Ellis widely discredited' www.blackbritain.co.uk

Gilroy, P. (2000) *between camps: nations, cultures and the allure of race London*: Penguin Books

Gilroy, P. (1987) *There Ain't No Black In The Union Jack* London: Hutchinson

Goldberg, D. T (1995), 'Polluting the body politic: Racist discourse and urban location', in M, Cross. and M, Keith. (eds) *Racism, the City and the State* London: Routledge

Graham, M. (2002) *Social Work And African Centred World Views* Birmingham: Venture Press

Grant, P. (2004) *Niggers Negroes Black People & Afrikans* Nottingham: Navigator Press

Griffin, J. (1984) *Black Like Me* London: Granada Books

Hall, S. & Bram, G. (1992) *Formations of Modernity: An Introduction to Sociology* London: Polity Press

Harris, C. (1993) Post-War Migration and the Industrial reserve Army' in James, W. & Harris, C. (eds) *Inside Babylon: The Caribbean Diaspora In Britain* London: Verso

Henry, W. A (2006) *What The Deejay Said: A Critique From The Street!* London: Learning By Choice Publications

Henry. W. A (2005) 'Projecting The Natural: Language, Citizenship and Representation In Outernational Culture' in Besson. J. & Olwig, K. F. (eds) *Caribbean Narratives of Belonging* London: Macmillan Press Ltd

Henry, W.A. (1996), 'Son, School and Father', The African Peoples Review, Reading: The International Institute for African Research, Vol IV, No 7, pp11-12.

Herrnstein, R. J. & Murray, C. (1996) *Bell Curve: Intelligence and Class Structure in American Life* USA: Free Press Paperbacks

hooks, b. (1996) *Killing Rage, Ending Racism* London: Penguin

Hurston, Z. N, (1990) 'My People! My People!' (in) Dundes, A. (1990) (ed) *Mother Wit from the Laughing Barrel* Jackson And London: University Of Mississippi Press.

Illich, I. D. (1971) *Deschooling Society* London: Calder & Boyars Ltd

Jensen, R. (2005) *The Heart of Whiteness: Confronting Race, Racism and White Privilege* San Francisco: City Lights Books

References

John, G. (2006) *Taking A Stand: Gus John Speaks on education, race, social action & civil unrest 1980-2005* Manchester, UK: Gus John Partnership Ltd

Jones, L. (1963) *Blues People* New York: Morrow Quill

Kuper, L. (1974) *Race Class And Power* London: G. Duckworth & Co Ltd

Lago, C. & Thompson, J. (1996) *Race, Culture, and Counseling* London: Open University Press

Lamming, G. (1986) *In the castle of my skin: with a critical introduction by David Williams* Harlow: Longman

Lazarre, J. (1997) *Beyond the Whiteness of Whiteness* Durham and London: Duke University Press

Leary, J. D. (2005) *Post Traumatic Slave Syndrome: America's Legacy of Enduring Injury and Healing* Milwaukie: Uptown Press

Liverpool, H. (2001) *Rituals Of Power And Rebellion: The Carnival tradition In Trinidad & Tobago 1763-1962* Chicago: Research Associates School Times Publication

Lezlee Lyrix (1983) 'Ghettotone Sound System' London

Lezlee Lyrix (1983) 'Just Be Cool'/'The Entertainer' (Disco 45) London: Ghettotone Record Label

Lezlee Lyrix (1989) 'Too Blak In Brixtain' (Demo Tape) London

Lezlee Lyrix (1994) 'Afrikan Body, White Man Mind' (Demo CD) London

Lezlee Lyrix (1994) 'Time To Make A Change' London: MCS Records

Martin. T (1986) *Race First: The Ideological and Organizational Struggles of Marcus Garvey and the Universal Negro Improvement Association* USA: The Majority Press

Mekoosha, M. (1993) 'The bodies politic – equality, difference and community practice' (in) Butcher, H., Glen, A., Henderson, P. & Smith, J. (eds) *Community and Public Policy* London: Pluto Press

McIntosh, P. (1990) 'White Privilege: Unpacking the Invisible Knapsack'. Reprinted from the Winter 1990 issue of Independent School

Miles. R (1982) *Racism and Migrant Labour* London: Routledge & Kegan Paul

Mullane, D. (1993) *Crossing The Danger Water: Three Hundred Years of African American Writing* New York: Doubleday

Nobles, W. & Goddard, L. L. (1984) *Understanding Black Family: A Guide For Scholarship And Research* California: Black Family Institute

Obinna, P. W. E. (2007) 'Making It Plainer' London: National Independent Education Coalition – www.niecoalition.org

References

Patterson, O. (1982) *The Sociology of Slavery* London: MacGibbon & Kee

Patterson. S (1964) *Dark Strangers* Bloomington: Indiana University Press

Pieterse, J. N. (1992) *White on black : images of Africa and blacks in western popular culture* London: Yale University Press in association with Cosmic Illusion Productions, Amsterdam

Public Enemy (1991) 'Burn Hollywood Burn' (Video) New York

Richardson, J. & Lambert, J. (1985) 'The Sociology of race' in Haralambos, M. (ed) *Sociology New Directions* Lancashire: Causeway Press

Rigby, Peter. (1996) *African Images: Racism And the end Of Anthropology* Oxford: Berg.

Rodney, W. (1969) *Groundings With My Brothers* London: Bogle-L' Overture

Rosaldo, R. (1989) *Culture and Truth: The Remaking of Social Analysis* London: Routledge

Scafe, S. (1989) *Teaching Black Literature* Virago Press Ltd, London

Schuyler, G. (1998) *Black No More Black Classics* London: X Press

Silk, G. (1996) 'Zion In A Vision Reggae Max Part 1' London: Jet Star

Sizzla (1994) 'True God' (45 White Label Single) Jamaica

Tate, S. (2002) 'Colour Matters, "Race" Matters: Afrikan Caribbean identity in the 21st Century' in Christian, M. (ed) *Black Identity in the 20th Century*: Expressions of the US and UK Afrikan Diaspora London: Hansib

Vertovec. S (1993) 'Indo-Caribbean Experience in Britain: Overlooked in James, W. & Harris, C. (eds) *Inside Babylon: The Caribbean Diaspora In Britain* London: Verso

Ware, V. & Back, L. (2002) *Out of Whiteness: Color, Politics and Culture* Chicago: University of Chicago Press

Welsing, F. C (1991) *The Isis Papers: The Keys to the Colors* Chicago: Third World Press

Woodson, C. G. (1993) *The Mis-education Of The Negro* USA: Africa World Press Inc.

Young. L (1996) *Fear of the Dark* London: Routledge